Helen
with warm regards
from

John

FREEDOM AND GRACE

FREEDOM AND GRACE

Essays by J. R. LUCAS

LONDON
SPCK

First published 1976
SPCK
Holy Trinity Church
Marylebone Road
London NW1 4DU

Thanks are due to the following for permission to quote from
copyright sources:

Oxford University Press: 'Pelagius and St Augustine',
first printed in the *Journal of Theological Studies* 1971

SCM Press Ltd: 'Childlike Morality', from *Christian Ethics and
Contemporary Philosophy*, ed. Ian Ramsey

Text set in 12 pt Photon Imprint, printed by photolithography,
and bound in Great Britain at The Pitman Press, Bath

ISBN 0 281 02932 6

To
B. G. M.

CONTENTS

AUTHOR'S PREFACE

If I had more time, I should rewrite these pieces into a coherent whole: but if I had had more time, they might never have been written at all. They are occasional pieces, occasioned sometimes by an argument with a friend or with myself, sometimes by a meeting of the Metaphysicals, sometimes to provide a paper at someone's request. Often they were written in a rush, and often I would have liked to mull over them, and work out much more fully what I was trying to say and what objections I needed to meet, and I grudge the tutorials and seminars and committee meetings which prevented me from following up ideas while they were fresh in my mind. But equally, without the stimulus of particular arguments in particular contexts, I might never have been moved to articulate my own views at all, and it was other men's disagreement that led me to develop arguments in favour of positions I had half-consciously taken up but had never adequately maintained or defended. I owe a great debt of gratitude to the members of the Metaphysicals, and especially Basil Mitchell, Helen Oppenheimer, Austin Farrer, Eric Mascall, and Ian Crombie, who regularly controverted my views, and made me think afresh. Philosophy is fertilized by difference of opinion.

Although differently occasioned, the papers have some common themes and are set against a particular intellectual background. The philosophical climate in which I grew up in Oxford was one of extreme aridity. An ability not to be convinced was the most powerful part of a young philosopher's armoury: a competent tutor could disbelieve any proposition, no matter how true it was, and the more sophisticated could not even understand the meaning of what was being asserted. In consequence, concern was concentrated on basic questions of epistemology almost to the exclusion of other questions of larger import but less easy to argue about in black and white terms. The undergraduate who wanted to write essays on the meaning of existence was told to confine himself to the logical grammar of 'is', and was not even allowed to ask what truth was, or how one ought to live one's life. I found it difficult to believe that questions many people wanted to ask were nonetheless meaningless, and never supposed that the profundities of philosophy could be settled by the niceties of English usage. I did not believe that phenomenalism was either meaningless or true; and equally I was sure that people, myself and others, existed, and could feel real pains and have real thoughts even though there was no overt behaviour or physiological phenomenon to prove it. But I did not feel free to assume it. Many philosophers, apparently well thought of, denied it. And so it seemed incumbent to labour simple points, and argue lengthily to prove the obvious. At the end of this period I remember reckoning that I had not discovered many new truths but had discovered that many old truths were really true.

I was much moved by Kant's *dictum* that the unavoidable problems of pure reason were God, freedom, and immortality, and it became evident to me that of these freedom was the one I should tackle first, partly as being the least inaccessible to human reason, and partly because I had long been turning over one argument in favour of freedom since I stumbled on it while still at school. It was clear that the freedom of the will, like most problems of philosophy and morals, was not a pseudo-problem but a real one, to which the right solution should be sought and could, perhaps, be found. And I was obstinately convinced that there was something special about people, that they could not be explained or understood merely as highly complicated animals, that personality existed in a category of its own. My argument was a very mathematical one which lies outside the scope of this book. It has proved very controversial. I have not yet succeeded in establishing it to the satisfaction of most philosophers, but I am fairly sure that the point I am trying to make is a valid one, and hope one day to be able to articulate it clearly enough to convince all my colleagues. Those who are interested can find my original paper, 'Minds, Machines and Gödel', in *Philosophy* XXXVI, 1961, pp. 112–27 (reprinted in Kenneth M. Sayre and Frederick J. Crosson, eds., *The Modeling of Mind*, Notre Dame 1963, pp. 255–71; and in Alan Ross Anderson, ed., *Minds and Machines*, Englewood Cliffs 1964, pp. 43–59); and more fully in my book, *The Freedom of the Will*, Oxford 1970.

The importance of personality and the intimations of objective truth have remained with me, and constitute two central themes in the first three papers. The problem of freedom and grace came out of my attempts to tackle the freedom of the will. I wrote the first draft in the autumn of 1960, and it went through many recensions, as I came more and more to distinguish personal relationships from moral and legal ones. It was finally published under the title 'Pelagius and St Augustine' in the *Journal of Theological Studies*, N.S., Vol. XXII, Pt. 1, April 1971, in a slightly different form. Here it stands with parts of two other papers on grace from the early 1960s in which I try to capture St Paul's insight into the way in which Christ has enabled us to have new life and be at one with God, but express it in the clinical terms of conceptual analysis rather than with the impassioned, but obscure, eloquence the apostle used himself.

Throughout the 1960s I was much occupied with the relation between God's activity and the created world. It was partly that if physical determinism was true, there was no room for any new initiative on God's part; but even if physical determinism was false, there was still an apparent conflict between man's freedom and God's intervention in human affairs. The tension between freedom and grace had been resolved by elucidating the concept of grace, and showing that properly understood it described God's attitude rather than his overt actions. But this left other problems still pressing; the paper on Providence deals with some of them. 'Rogationtide Queries' came to me during a sermon at Evensong in Exeter Cathedral on Rogation Sunday, 1963. I have revised it considerably, and incorporate here some arguments which also appear in my *Freedom of the Will*, as well as an attempt to answer a point put to me by A. R. W. Harrison, then Warden of Merton, that so long as man has free-will there is a perpetual possibility of his frustrating any plans God may have for him or for others. It is a problem I had skirted round in 'Freedom and Grace' and 'Providence'; here I attempt to resolve it by conceding the infinite vulnerability of the Christian God, while maintaining also his infinite flexibility and capacity of making fresh approaches.

'The Origin of Sin' was written for Merton College Church Society in 1961. I intended at the time to continue with a sequel on the Redemption, but did not get round to writing it until late in 1972. The paper on Reasons for Loving and Being Loved was written in Trinity Term 1973 to summarize and carry on a discussion at the Metaphysicals. In it I try to reconcile the freedom and spontaneity that are the marks of a personal relationship with the rationality and objectivity we ascribe to God, and distinguish different senses of reason, a first-personal sense of reasons I adopt, and a second-personal sense of reasons I urge on you as cogent and leaving you no alternative but to act in the way laid down.

I am not entirely happy with the theory of punishment put forward in 'Or Else', originally published in the *Proceedings of the Aristotelian Society*, LXIX, 1968–9, pp. 207–22, and have therefore not reprinted it here. It does not do justice to retributivism. There are, in fact, several different retributive elements in most people's thinking, and they need a fuller and deeper treatment than I have given them. They are much more closely linked with repentance and forgiveness than people like to think, and I do not think I shall be able to be clear about punishment until I have thought my way through the Christian doctrine of forgiveness. One of the papers printed here was originally published in *Theology*, 1971, pp. 194–200, and is a review of *Marriage, Divorce, and the Church*, the report of the Commission on the Christian Doctrine of Marriage, which I had had to discuss as a member of the Archbishop's Commission on Christian Doctrine. In its deliberations, I, along with the other members of the Commission, have often been called upon to produce working papers. These often embody the thoughts of other members, but seldom succeed in satisfying them all, and seldom therefore have seen the light of day. In publishing the ones included here, I both extend my thanks to those whose thoughts I have plagiarized, and explain that my exposition of them does not carry any corporate endorsement by the Commission of what I have said.

The two papers on Christian morality date from the early 1960s. Some time in 1961 I read in the *Times Literary Supplement* a brief notice of Professor Nowell-Smith's paper, 'Morality: Religious and Secular', in the current issue of the *Rationalist Annual*, in which the reviewer said that unless the Christians could meet the charges there made, they might as well go out of business. And so, as soon as I was free in the Long Vac, I made it my first concern to obtain a copy of his paper, and write a reasoned reply to it. I offered it to the *Rationalist Annual*, but, quite reasonably, they felt it was not incumbent on them to publish Christian argumentation, and it was only some years later that Ian Ramsey, who had heard it read at the Metaphysicals, asked if he could have it as a companion piece for Nowell-Smith's paper which he was reprinting in his *Cristian Ethics and Contemporary Philosophy* (SCM 1966). The other paper, 'Christian Morality', was written for a Roman Catholic society in Merton in 1961.

The remaining papers are occasional pieces that are self-explanatory. More important than what is included is what is lacking. The bearing of the Christian insights into the personal nature of man upon our moral and social philosophy needs far more systematic working out than I have been able to give it. In other books, *The Principles of Politics* (Oxford 1966) and *Democracy and Participation* (Penguin 1976), I have attempted to bring some of these insights to bear on political philosophy, but there I am not concerned with specifically Christian approaches. Christians, aware of the fallibility of man, need to set their political thought in a minor key, being more concerned to minimize the greatest evils than to aspire to the greatest goods, which, if they are to be achieved at all, must be achieved by other than political means. Politics, for the Christian, is the resolute pursuit of the least bad, and therefore the characteristic flowering of the Christian life will be found not in the purely political realm but elsewhere. The Christian Member of Parliament or civil servant will be illumined in his judgements by his understanding of the realities of human nature and the ultimate values of human life, but few of his professional decisions will be straightforward exemplifications of the Sermon on the Mount. The same holds good, to a lesser extent, of the business man, the doctor, the teacher, and even the minister of religion. We need to think much harder how a twentieth-century Christian can be in the world but not of it.

The other main deficiency is in the intellectual justification of the faith. God is not simply the Way or the Life, but is also the Truth, and although the schoolmen were wrong to talk of an *ens realissimum*, and ought rather to have approached him as *Abba*, Father, nevertheless we need to maintain also that he must be *realissimus* too. God is not just a figment of our imagination, but exists quite independently of whether or not we worship him; and although we are left free to decide whether to or not, it is not an arbitrary decision which each man may make as his fancy pleases, but one which is weighty and which must be pondered and reasoned about. There are many different senses of the word 'reason', and it is entirely understandable why, in some of those senses, Christian thinkers have wanted to deny that Christianity was a matter of rational assessment and have wanted to claim that the faith transcends all reason. But we should not, if we take St John's prologue seriously, construe reason in such a confined sense that it cannot be identified with God. We must allow rationality to God or we deny his truth. And therefore also we must consider the intellectual content of the Christian religion, and the arguments that may be adduced both for and against it. It is no easy matter, and often in this present age the Christian thinker may be called on to wrestle with doubt. But every thinker who is serious about thinking has to make up his mind about what the universe is really like and what are the ultimate values that we should seek. An academic suspension of belief is not a course that can remain always open to us. And in the last paper I sketch the alternatives, as I see them, to belief in a personal God.

Michaelmas 1975   J. R. LUCAS

1 FREEDOM AND GRACE[1]

Christians are often equivocal in their attitude to freedom. On the one hand, they are firmly for it, because they believe in the moral responsibility of the individual, and freedom is a prerequisite of moral responsibility. On the other hand, believing in a theocentric universe, they want to ascribe everything to God and see him as the sole and sufficient cause of all events.

I shall argue in favour of the former view. For one thing, I am convinced that a certain freedom of the will *is* a necessary condition of moral responsibility. The current arguments in favour of determinism without tears, which maintain that there is no conflict between determinism and our normal ascriptions of responsibility, are to my mind not at all cogent. The considerations which have led theologians to push theocentricity to the exclusion of freedom are also not compelling. And finally, the view of God that Christ has shown us, is one in which God, as father, would want us, as his children, to be free: and I am more inclined to doubt the logic of those who argue that this is not the case, than the veracity of those who report Christ as having revealed that it is.

The issue was first fought out between Pelagius and St Augustine. It is one of the few serious disputes where linguistic analysis can help. The question turns on the group of concepts around 'cause', 'explanation', and 'responsible'. St Augustine, in giving an account of his career, was right to say that not unto him should be ascribed the glory, but unto God. It was no triumph of the natural Augustine that the pagan professor became a Christian bishop. St Augustine, like St Paul, kicked hard against the pricks, and it was only the relentless pressure of God's will that brought him to accept God's plan for his life, instead of his own. Yet Pelagius was right too, to protest that St Augustine's language, if taken literally, denied the manhood of God's children, and, in allowing them no mind of their own, put them on a par with sticks and stones. But Pelagius in his turn said more than he should. Where St Augustine had made man into a mere thing,

[1] A slightly different version of this chapter was published in the *Journal of Theological Studies*, N.S., Vol. XXII, Pt. 1 (April 1971), under the title 'Pelagius and St Augustine'.

Pelagius in restoring man, was on the way to making a mere thing of God. St Augustine had been right to ascribe the credit not to himself but to God, wrong to seem to say that he himself had had no say in whether he would do God's will or not. Pelagius was right to stress man's freedom, wrong to convert autonomy into autarky, and freedom into pride.

We can conveniently exhibit the root of these errors in terms of the concept 'cause'. This concept is under tension. Part of its sense is straining towards the ideal of a *complete* cause, part towards that of *most significant* cause. If we are asked what was the cause of a man's acting in a certain way, we can give a short answer, but we realize that that does not finish the matter. Our interrogator can ask further questions, or we may anticipate his questions, and give an extended account which will answer them in advance. Any short assessment of causes, however just, is, we feel, incomplete: and we have an ideal of a complete causal account, which will take nothing for granted and which will leave no room for further questioning by a reasonable man. So undergraduates write lengthy essays on the causes of the First World War, so St Augustine writes in full of the causes of his conversion to Christianity, so Newman writes of the causes of his secession to Rome. But as we gratify the urge to completeness, we become conscious of another, contrary, urge, an urge to summarize and select some factors as being more important or more significant than others. Thucydides writes of the causes of the Peloponnesian War, and devotes a whole book to giving a fairly full account, yet finds himself impelled to summarize it all and say in a sentence what the *real cause*, the *alēthestatē prophasis*, was.

It is not only brevity that impels us to give short answers. We often need to pick out one factor above all others as being *the* cause, because this is the one most within our control, or because this was the most abnormal factor, or because this was the action most deserving of praise or blame. The motives behind our selection are somewhat complex, and the criteria we use are exceedingly complex. This is not the place to offer a full account of either. Enough for our present purpose that part of the sense of the word 'cause' demands that we select *one* causal factor as being *the* cause.

It will help to make my argument clear if we consider the paradigm case of causes, the causes of natural phenomena in the world of inanimate objects. Many people believe that these are the only causes, properly speaking; so much so that the word 'cause' and more especially the adjective 'causal' has acquired something of that sense, and we mean by 'causal explanation' an explanation in terms of this type of cause and not any other. This view, I believe, is wrong, and is a further source of confusion, leading philosophers to misunderstand personal relations in general, and God's grace towards men in particular. The explanation we offer of natural phenomena is not the only possible type of explanation. Nevertheless, it is a very clear one for the illustration of the different meanings of the word 'cause'.

The full causal explanation of a natural phenomenon is given in terms of a natural uniformity and an antecedent sufficient condition. The natural uniformity is usually not stated but only implied. The antecedent sufficient condition is often not stated in full either. Although we sometimes feel that to give the cause of any phenomenon, we must state the minimum antecedent sufficient condition in full, we normally pick out only one or two factors as being the cause. This is because the minimum antecedent sufficient condition in full is usually complicated, and includes a large number of *standing conditions* and *negative conditions*, which it would be tedious to spell out in full. Striking a match will cause it to ignite, but only provided that the match is struck in an atmosphere containing oxygen—matches struck in helium do not ignite. Putting down the switch will cause the light to go on, but only provided that the bulb has not burnt out, the fuses have not blown, the wiring is not defective, and there is no power cut. We do not normally specify these standing or negative conditions, because we can normally take them for granted, and it would be tedious and unnecessary to detail them; but if occasion arose, or if we were pressed on the point, we would at once agree that without these conditions the phenomenon would not have occurred —hence the lawyers' term *'conditiones sine qua non'*. They are undoubtedly part of the minimum sufficient condition, and therefore are part of the cause in its wider sense, and when we are pressed by a questioner, or are trying to be careful on our own account, we take this to be the real meaning of the word 'cause'; but otherwise, for adequate pragmatic reasons, *conditiones sine qua non* are distinguished from, rather than considered part of, *'the* cause'. Moreover, from different points of view different causal

3

factors will be selected as '*the* cause' without there being any contradiction involved. What cannot change without contradiction is the full specification of the minimum antecedent sufficient condition; but which constituent factor it is worth mentioning depends on who the speaker is, to whom he is speaking, what their common interests are, and what their common assumptions are. The coroner will say the cause of death was drowning, the unsuccessful rescuer will think the cause was his failure to dive well enough, the teenage chum will know that it was his folly in having dared his friend to swim to the wreck, the mother that it was having let him go out swimming on such a nasty cold day, the father that it was his having failed to instil more sense and more moral courage into his head. Each singles out a different cause: but there is no disagreement on any question of substance.

St Augustine uses 'cause' in its narrower sense. He is concerned to ascribe credit, not to exhibit antecedent sufficient conditions, and, the cast of his thought being theocentric throughout, his ascriptions of credit are always to God. Since an ominipotent God always could have disposed affairs differently, and always could have intervened to prevent a particular person acting in a particular way, it is a *negative* condition of the occurrence of any event, that God did not decide to prevent its occurring; but whereas most of us are ready to record this with an unemphatic *Deo volente*, St Augustine is half inclined to stress God's acquiescence in the course of events as the most significant condition of their occurring, and therefore as the cause.

This is only a tendency in St Augustine. Often there is much more to his ascriptions than a semi-vacuous emphasis on *Deo volente*. In recalling his own passage through life, he is struck by the relentless, though ever gentle, pressure of God's quest for him. Nourished though he was on Christianity with his mother's milk, he had not accepted it, nor had he been converted by some sudden wonder wrought before his eyes, which left him no option but to believe. It was, rather, that he could not get away from the problem of God, and that wherever he went, Carthage or Rome, Ostia or Milan, he had not gone from God's spirit or his presence, and that whatever intellectual position he adopted, paganism or Manicheeism, the superficial piety of Cicero or the bottomless obscurities of the Neoplatonists, he could not make his abode there long, and could not be content until he had reached him in whom there is rest and an end of journeyings.

This is a non-vacuous and entirely proper use of the word 'cause'. We often pick out as '*the* cause' that factor which will, sooner or later, if not in conjunction with one factor then in conjunction with another, bring about the final result. Thus Thucydides, in giving as the cause of the Peloponnesian War Sparta's jealousy of Athens' growing power, means to say that the war might have been triggered off as well by Corcyra or Potidea as by Aegina, and that if matters had been patched up in 431, there would still have been trouble in 429 or 428, or anyhow in 427 over Mytilene. So too the wooer, if he cannot win the heart of the beloved by skill at tennis, takes dancing lessons, and if she is still not in the mood to say Yes at the end of a ball, will see what a skiing holiday will do. So too God, in seeking Augustine's soul, if he will not heed the simple faith of Monnica, will unleash the intellectual force of Ambrose, and if he will not obey admonitions heard in public in church, will speak to him in private in the garden.

It is easy in retrospect to see events, particularly those that constitute one's own life, as more inevitable than they really are. Although in picking out one underlying factor as the cause, we are committed to the belief that, even if other circumstances had been somewhat different, one way or another the event in question would have come to pass, we are not committed to saying that the event could not but have come to pass. History is full of the inevitable not happening. If Sennacherib had captured Jerusalem or Hitler conquered England, historians would have explained the causes, and many would have made it seem inevitable in each case. But this is an illusion, stemming from the other sense of the word 'cause'. If one means by 'cause' 'antecedent sufficient condition' then causes must inevitably be followed by their effects. But where one is using 'cause' to mean not 'antecedent sufficient condition' but only 'most important member of the set of conditions that are conjointly sufficient', then no inevitability is involved, not even in the cases where the most important condition has been selected because there is a wide range of other conditions in conjunction with which it will bring about the events in question. St Augustine might feel that it was God's seeking him, rather than any action of his own, that was responsible for his conversion to Christianity, and could justify this ascription of responsibility by recounting how his many attempts to escape from God had proved fruitless, and how one way and another he was constantly being brought to consider the claims of Christianity and its demands on his own life. But while the pattern of St Augustine's life justifies his saying that it was on account of God's seeking him that he became a Christian, and was not due to any innate niceness of his own, it does not follow that Augustine could not have resisted God's search for his allegiance. Ahab also had the feeling that God was looking for him.

It is always possible to say No. It is a right that God has conferred, *vis-à-vis* himself, on both halves of mankind. The cost in unhappiness, frustration, or futility may be beyond all reckoning, but if we are determined to have our own way, at whatever cost, rather than his, then we can. Those who have said Yes may not be able, on looking back, to believe that they ever could have said No, and indeed to have done so would have been to deny their proper development; but they could have said No nonetheless, and it seems that some people actually do. Pelagius was right to insist on this; for God being the God he has shown us that he is, and man being what he has made him, man's decision is an essential part of the antecedent sufficient condition of his own actions. One may, on grounds similar to St Augustine's, or for other reasons, ascribe to God the credit for one's actions; and one may use the word 'cause' in its selective sense to do this: but it remains true nonetheless, that those actions were done by oneself, and that one could have not done them, and that a full causal account must include one's own decision as an essential factor; in the wider sense of 'cause', a human decision is a necessary part of the cause of a human action; or if we take the selective sense, and say that the *causa causans* was the operation of God, yet a *conditio sine qua non* was the co-operation of oneself.

It might seem that in saying this much, we had said too much. If we insist on the agent's being in effective control of his actions, then must not he alone be described as the cause? The answer is No. Although the agent's decision is a necessary condition of the actions being performed, it is not sufficient condition. That the circumstances should be favourable is also a necessary condition. Situated as I am in Oxford, I can spend the next twenty minutes walking round Christ Church Meadows, if I so decide, but I cannot this morning walk round the Cambridge Backs. Decisions are not taken in a vacuum. Even though human beings are free to choose between alternatives, not every course of action is open to them, nor of those that are open to them are all equally reasonable to adopt. And therefore the sufficient condition of an action's being performed is not just the agent's sole decision, but a conjunction of other circumstances with his decision; and of this causal complex we may well select some other factor than the agent's decision as being the most significant factor. Thus we can perfectly well acknowledge the freedom of the will and continue using causal language, ascribing causes of actions not to the agent's own choice but to other considerations or circumstances, or even to other people.

We are so ready to regard one person as having been the cause of another's actions, that our whole language is shaped to fit. In ordinary life, we are all familiar with one person's putting another up to do something, and in such cases we regard the one as much responsible as the other for what was done. Often, in fact, we will speak of one as having 'done' what strictly speaking the other actually did. Indeed, outside the textbooks of the moral philosophers, the word 'agent' means a person who acts for another, not for himself, and the principal is deemed to have done whatever the agent has performed in his name. When we speak of Justinian's Digest, we do not wish to be understood as denying the labours of the lawyers who actually did the compilation: we call it Justinian's, or say that he compiled it, because he *caused* it to be compiled, that is, gave instructions to others to do it. In the same way we speak of Solomon's having built the temple, though it is doubtful whether with his own hands he so much as placed one stone upon another. Thus our ordinary way of speaking allows us to talk not only of one person's having caused the actions of another, but of his having done them; and we find no difficulty in ordinary life in holding more than one person responsible for the same action, both the serpent who put them up to it, and Adam and Eve for actually eating the forbidden fruit.

As with our discourse about men, so with our discourse about God: we can ascribe to God the responsibility for man's actions without thereby denying man's responsibility too. There is no inconsistency in saying that God was responsible for Augustine's conversion, and that Augustine was. The inconsistency would arise only if we tried to say that both were primarily responsible.

7

And if in this case we say that God was primarily responsible, this still does not mean that Augustine was not responsible at all, was not free to say No, any more than when we say that Baden-Powell was primarily responsible for the Boy Scout movement, we are thereby denying freedom to all who supported him.

Thus an easy resolution seems possible in the dispute between Pelagius and St Augustine: we can allow to Pelagius what he is standing out for, namely human freedom, while conceding to St Augustine that it is nevertheless God who is primarily responsible for man's turning away from error and towards truth. God, having limited himself in conferring free-will on some of his creatures, is not the sole, sufficient, and complete cause of human action; so Pelagius, rightly. God the creator of the world and redeemer of mankind, is the initiator of all those actions wherein we do well, and is the cause of our being saved; so St Augustine, rightly. A simple solution, turning on the two meanings of the word 'cause'.

This is a solution, but it is only half a solution. Many difficulties have been generated by confusion over the concept of cause and similar concepts, and these can be resolved by a clarification of the concepts involved. Nevertheless, difficulties still remain, and though the somewhat Pelagian account outlined above is, so far as it goes, true, it is only half true, and St Augustine was right in denouncing the consequences implicit in Pelagius' statement of his position.

We can approach the difficulties that still remain by remarking that St Augustine's experience is not a universal one, and that for some people God was not '*the* cause' of their salvation in exactly the same way that he was of St Augustine's or St Paul's. Some people have no sense of seeking for or being sought by God, because they have always known him and always trusted him: people brought up from their infancy as Christians, who have grown up in faith, and, though they have had their temptations and their failures, have never had serious doubts, and never been separated from the body of the Church. Such people cannot know the persistent pressure of God's will, because they have not resisted it enough. A loyal and faithful churchman, who makes his communion every Sunday, reads his Bible every day, and says his prayers morning and evening, does not naturally exclaim 'Whither then shall I go from thy presence?' even though he knows his efforts are too feeble and his lapses too frequent. In like case is the young man brought up by agnostic parents, who when he comes up to the university decides to give the claims of Christianity careful consideration, and after going through them, and weighing all the factors in his mind, concludes that they are true, and commits himself thereafter to the Christian life. Without kicking against them, one cannot feel the pricks: and though such people may still ascribe their salvation to Christ, they cannot do so in quite the same sense as St Augustine did, because they cannot have the same sense of having had all their movements away from God countered by the finger of providence.

Of course, if we give a *complete* causal account of a man's being, or becoming, a Christian, it is at once obvious that he is not the sole and sufficient cause of his salvation, but that God's antecedent actions were a prerequisite, and that therefore it is as much God's doing as his own. No theist would deny that God is omnipotent, and that he could intervene to prevent any particular event's occurring, and that therefore his non-intervention is a necessary condition of each event. Both as Creator of the world and as non-intervener in particular cases, God's will is an essential part of every cause in the wide sense. Nevertheless, there are subtle logical pressures which make for pride. We are loath, for good reason, to describe God's creation or his non-intervention as '*the* cause', in the narrow sense, of each event. The reason is that to do so would fail to distinguish between different causes of different events. We feel that there is something vacuous in adding *Deo volente* to every prediction and every causal statement, because if it is to be *said* always, we could equally well *understand* it always, leaving it unsaid. Rome fell, we say, because God did not intervene to save it. But if Rome had not fallen, we should equally ascribe that to God's non-intervention, in the same way as we do ascribe its survival in previous centuries to God's forbearance. That is, whether Rome falls or not, God is the cause. But this, though true , tells us nothing of those factors accessible to human minds, which differentiate the occasion of Rome's falling from the occasions on which it was preserved.

The difficulty is one common to all theology and metaphysics. Human language is shaped by the needs of natural men in the world of nature. It is suited for communication between men about practical affairs, not for praise or adoration or discourse

9

about God. In particular, our ordinary purposes demand that we should always be distinguishing feature from feature and circumstance from circumstance, whereas in our metaphysical moments we are seeking to express the underlying unity of reality and the unchangingness of God. The theocentric purposes of St Augustine are gainsaid by the *nisus* of ordinary speech. He may wish to ascribe all credit to God, but there is a tendency built into the sense of the word 'cause' to pick out as *the* cause a factor that is peculiar to the effect.

The conditions of God's creation of the world and non-intervention in it are too general, and in the latter case too negative, to be naturally taken as causes of events: God's action as Redeemer of mankind has come to be in like case. The early Christian converts, Cornelius or Lydia, would have had no hesitation in ascribing their salvation to the direct action of God, in sending his apostles, Peter and Paul, to bring them the good tidings. Their experience was different from that of St Augustine or St Paul, but nonetheless such as to make them feel that God had sought them out, and it was by no action of their own but by his favour that they had been brought to the knowledge of the truth. The very success of evangelism since apostolic times has destroyed this. Even in St Augustine's days the gospel was no longer news, and now, just as the clergy are felt to be not so much emissaries as fixtures, so the claims of the Christian religion are part of the background of the intellectual scene, and the impression of having been singled out cannot be as strong in an age of wayside pulpits and Agreed Syllabuses as in the time when the whole people walked in darkness. A man may still give thanks for having been born of the parents that he was born of, and having been at the school that he was at, and for having had the friends, and heard the sermons, and known the pastors, that he had; and yet there were others situated as he was, who chose otherwise. Two were in the field; the one was taken and the other left.

Thus although no serious Christian could think of his own vocation as other than dependent on the saving activity of God in sending his Son to live among us, to tell us what was in the Father's mind and vouch for his veracity with his life, and in vindicating divine omnipotence by the resurrection, yet there is a continuous pressure to talk of this as the *conditio sine qua non*, and to take the *causa causans* to be his own response to God's call.

Nor is this altogether wrong. We often select as the cause the most variable factor among those constituting the antecedent sufficient condition. It is the weakest link in a chain that attracts our attention, not the strongest. God is unfailing, only man can fail. If God's scheme for man's salvation is brought to nought, it will be due to man, not God: and therefore if man is saved, it will, in view of God's unvarying love, be because man proved worthy of his salt.

A perilously short distance separates this position from that of pride. The cause may sometimes be selected as the most variable factor, but it is sometimes selected as the most important one, and often carries with it an ascription of praise. The old Adam in us will lose no opportunity of congratulating himself on his spiritual excellence in saying Yes, where the stiff-necked had refused to signify assent: the weakest link takes credit for not actually breaking, while the story of God's redemption of mankind is taken as read.

It is not only, however, a case of pride making use of opportunities that logic offers; logic also is at fault. The logic of causality is too much modelled on the causes of natural phenomena, the world of things put in subjection under man's feet. Causes (in the narrow sense) are largely selected from the point of view of a manipulator, what one would have to do in order to bring about a certain result. This applies well enough to things. It is one of the fundamental facts about the world we live in that we can select means which will be effective in bringing about ends, irrespective of most other factors. Most factors are causally irrelevant to a given causal connection. If it were not so—if most experiments could not be reproduced irrespective of the colour of the sky— natural science and our common-sense concept of cause would be impossible. In particular, mental attitudes are characteristically irrelevant to the success of our manipulations. Fire burns whether I will it or not: I need only add a drop of sulphuric acid to a mixture of sugar and potassium chlorate, and however insolent or arrogant my attitude may be, there will be an explosion all the same. With God, however, the logic of thingly causality does not apply. When we are dealing with things, it is reasonable and right to avert our attention from those standing conditions which, though necessary, are always satisfied, and concentrate on what remains to be done if the desired result is to be effected. The one

11

we can reasonably take for granted: it is the other that we have to change. But God we may not take for granted: he is a person, not a thing: there can be no technique for manipulating him.

St Paul's antithesis between justification by faith and justification by works could be rendered in modern terms as the insight that salvation depended on one's attitude and was not a matter of technique. It follows from God's being a person. Because he is a person, we cannot hope that he can be secured by anything less than a whole-hearted approach. A grudging observance of the law of nature is enough to secure domination over nature, but a grudging reception of the sacraments or a prudential observance of some moral law will not win the love of God any more than it will the love of a human being. There is the same absurdity in supposing that there was anything one could do that would automatically cause God to accept one, as there would be in believing that one had a sure-fire way of winning a woman's heart: the very fact that one believed this would vitiate all that one did. If we hope one day to know even as we are known, and to be with God face to face, it could not conceivably be otherwise than by his favour, his special personal favour extended to each one of us, since all personal relations are by personal favour, and not of right nor mechanically determined. But in this life most of us are so far from God, that we tend to impersonalize him, and need to be corrected of that error.

Although God is a person, and his favour therefore not to be presumed upon, he is not fickle as humans all too often are, nor is he arbitrary, notwithstanding what St Augustine and Calvin were tempted to say. Knock and it shall be opened unto you: none who wholeheartedly seek the Lord shall be in any wise cast out. Although he could withhold his favour, he does not. He is not to be taken for granted, but he can be relied upon. So that although it is a deadly error to treat God as a thing, it is a saving truth to ascribe to God that permanence we ordinarily associate with things rather than persons. Our God is not a stick or stone to be handled as we please: nevertheless he is a Rock, on whom we may surely build all our hopes. He does not change in his love for us: only we do, in our love for him. If we will have him, we can be sure that he will have us. The choice is ours, Pelagius is right. Only, it is not thanks to us the choice is ours, but thanks to God: we could not have sought him, unless he had first sought us. And only a whole-hearted response to his call will avail us anything. We cannot accept God's invitation to the wedding feast, but go in our ordinary clothes.

The philosophically-minded Christian must make a reconciliation between Pelagius and St Augustine in some such way as that of the account offered here. Believing in human freedom, as a Christian must, he cannot refuse to speak in the first person. I did it: I could have done otherwise, but I chose to do it. But as soon as he has said this, he has said too much, arrogating to himself a credit that is God's, and speaking as though he were of himself sufficient to obtain his own salvation: so he goes on to say at once 'Yet not I, but God in me', and attributes all to the grace of God rather than himself, meaning by the grace of God all those factors which he recognizes as having been at work in his own conversion and pilgrimage, apart from himself. Grace is thus a negative concept. It is the noun corresponding to the 'Yet not I' of the Christian's disavowal of credit. It will therefore vary in content from man to man. One will see it as the relentless pressure of circumstance that turned him to God, another in the sudden and inexplicable surge of support that enabled him to overcome temptation, a third in the voice of God, speaking directly to him in his own heart, a fourth in the mediation of the gospel to him through the mouth of another, parent, parson, teacher, or friend. It is scarcely surprising that, with its many differing applications, and with our natural tendency to assume '*Unum nomen, unum nominatum*', the word 'grace' has generated confusion among Christian thinkers.

Thus far we have achieved clarification by analysis of the different senses of certain key words, such as 'cause'. But there is a deeper source of confusion and distortion than unclearness about the meanings of words. There is a tension between the programme of complete explicability we all subscribe to and the requirements of freedom. If men have free-will, then complete explanations of their decisions cannot be given. This does not mean, as some philosophers seem to have persuaded themselves, that free decisions are arbitrary. If we want to know why a man decided as he did, we can give his reasons. In almost all cases he will have reasons, so that his action is not arbitrary. But what we cannot give is the reason why he is in fact reasonable, and decides in favour of the most reasonable rather than some other course.

Reasons by themselves do not—could not—necessitate a man's decision in any determinist sense, nor do they afford the type of *complete* explanation we are tempted to demand. We can explain actions all right, that is, give those reasons that the agent, if perfectly honest, would offer for his actions, but we cannot explain the agent's being a rational agent, in so far as he is one. We can explain men's failure to be rational, but not their conformity to the standards of rationality. This is just a fortunate fact, that our Creator made us not barely two-legged animals but, although imperfectly, rational as well. But this is not answer enough for a complete explanation, because, being free, we always can, and often do, choose to disregard the weight of reason, and choose some other course than that which is reasonable and right. And this, the fundamental fact of freedom, seems mysterious, Two men in the field, one shall be taken and one left. It is a mystery. Two people may have the gospel preached to them in the same way, and have the same opportunities of hearing God's call for each, and one may hearken and the other harden his heart. We ask 'Why?' No answer can be given except that the one decided to, and the other not to. This is the point where there has to be an end of answering. Just as in some determinist pictures of the universe, where we explain events in terms of initial conditions, we are asked why the state of the universe at the beginning of time was what it was, and have to admit that no explanation can be given of this—it just was the case and that is all there is to be said—, so in any libertarian view of the universe, questions can be asked but cannot be answered, why free agents chose to act in a rational fashion, and not in some other way. We cannot answer such questions: but we may be tempted to go through the forms of answering. Asked why I acted, I give my reasons: asked why I chose to accept them as reasons, I can properly say only 'I just did', but pressed for an explanation, and not realizing that this is a point where no further explanation can be offered, I am tempted to escape from the ultimateness of my decision, and say 'I suppose I am made that way'. And the Christian, having to hand the elastic concept of grace, and being predisposed to ascribe everything to the Almighty, goes further and says 'God made me the sort of person who would do this' or, simply, 'God, by his grace, made me do it'. But this is wrong. It denies the fatherhood of God. God does not *make* us do things. His way are ways of gentleness, not of

14

compulsion or force. He could have made us potter's vessels, but he has in fact made us men: we are his creatures, but his children too, free, capable of being reasonable, capable of hearkening to his voice, but capable also of being wrong, capable of hardening our hearts. That we can come to know God and love him, through the rationality with which he has endowed us, through the saving actions of his Son and the activity of the Church, and through the particular counsel and support vouchsafed to us by the Holy Spirit on various occasions, are all matters of grace, marks of divine favour, for which we owe no thanks to ourselves at all, but to God only: but the final decision, the final right of refusal, he has vested in us, and we, not God, are answerable for the answer we return.

2 THE NEW ST PAUL

If God is a person, it follows that our relations with God are personal relations. They are to be understood by analogy with our relations to human beings, not our relations with material objects, or numbers, or principles, or ideas. We can manipulate material objects, calculate numbers, adopt principles, comprehend ideas; but not persons.

Things can be manipulated, but men object to being pawns. Characteristically, personal relations are not manipulations, but the free persuasions of free minds: if we want to address ourselves to another human being, it is a matter not for our hands alone, but our whole heart. The aircraftsman on duty is apt to be slovenly. He is neither as smart nor as respectful as an army officer would like. This is because he is dealing with inanimate objects, and it does not matter whether his hair is unkempt or his manner insolent, so long as he connects up the right wires to the right terminals, and does just those things that the technical job requires. Provided that those things have been done, the aeroplane will fly, whether the technician was courteous and clean or the reverse. Not so, however, when the same man is off duty and courting his girl. Aeroplanes will perform as desired, irrrespective of one's general manner, but not girls. There are no techniques for manipulating human beings which are so much techniques that provided one has the expertise, it does not matter what attitude one manifests. One cannot limit oneself to certain factors only and let the rest go hang, as one can with inanimate objects: personal relations demand the whole man.

Some people, it is true, can succeed to some extent in manipulating their fellow men, but this reflects man's finitude, not his humanity. God, who is infinite, cannot be moved by any limited effort of man; and, knowing the secrets of all hearts, he cannot be deceived by any outward show we may put on. There can be no technique of manipulating him.

God is not a Thing. Nor is he an Idea. If we were Platonists, we might believe that there was some technique whereby we could emancipate ourselves from the shackles of our earthly existence and put ourselves on a level with the Forms. But God, being a living spirit, has a different sort of existence from the dead timelessness of the Forms. Knowledge of him is not like knowledge of mathematical truths, which any man can set himself to come to know, but like knowledge of persons, and is essentially an interchange between two parties, requiring not only our wish to know, but his willingness to be known.

Personal relations are by personal favour. They cannot be merited. But neither can they fail to be merited. It is a conceptual 'cannot'. We cannot either have or not have a right to be loved, because love is not the sort of thing about which it makes sense to ask legal or moral questions. This is not to say that we cannot ask legal or moral questions, but only that legal and moral questions define their own subject matter. Thus we can ask legal or moral questions about the justice of God, and can quite properly take exception to an account of God which makes him out to be an arbitrary and unjust despot. But when we say that salvation cannot be earned, or that we are all miserable sinners, this is not to say that God is being less fair than Pelagius would have been, or that our customary moral distinctions are all invalid, but is, rather, an obscure way of saying that justice, which we do indeed deserve, is not what we want, and that the only thing that we really want is something which if it is to be had at all must come spontaneously and unforcedly and not in consequence of any legal or moral obligation. The undergraduate who adduces twenty different reasons why Amaryllis ought to love him shows his ignorance of love. There are many things, no doubt, that Amaryllis ought to do—perhaps she ought to go with him to a Commem., having promised so to do: perhaps she ought to listen with courtesy to his expostulations, to let him explain how little she has understood him: certainly she should not treat him with disdain, or tease his jealous fears, or circulate his letters around Lady Margaret Hall. And perhaps many Amaryllises fail on these obligations, and perhaps the young man has just cause for complaint. But the keeping of obligations, although important, will never be enough. What one can oblige another to do will never satisfy the heart's desire. What comes of right is not that worth having, and what is ultimately worthwhile therefore can never be merited. When men do receive what is worth having they are often therefore overwhelmed with a sense of their being unworthy of it. But this is a logical truth about worth-i-ness, not a moral failure on the part of the men. The man who is in love and has his love returned may feel that he is a worm and utterly unworthy of the love of his beloved, but this is not because he is worse than other men, but because he sees himself, under the influence of love, as a person, not a bearer of legal or moral titles, and knows that between persons there are no titles and no obligations, and everything is, as it must be, unforced and free.

The conceptual truth that moral and legal categories do not apply to personal relations, is easily, but misleadingly, expressed in the material mode of speech, by saying simply that love, and in particular, God's love, is unmerited. For the Christian, to be loved by God is alone ultimately worthwhile. With it we are all right, whatever else befalls us: without it we are lost, whatever else we enjoy or achieve. To be loved by God is to be 'justified', *dikaiousthai*, is salvation. And then we say that salvation is not merited, and are taken to mean that salvation is unmerited, and that God has arbitrarily chosen some people to go to heaven and have a good time for ever and ever, Amen, and others to go to burn, probably for ever and ever, Amen, too.

The mistake has been two-fold. We have expressed the conceptual truth that love is not the sort of thing that can or can fail to be merited, by the contingent false assertion that though it conceivably might be, it is not in fact bestowed according to merit. And we have understood salvation in Mohammedan rather than Christian terms, as some pleasant physical state rather than anything to do with personal relations. God could have been a just God, but has chosen to be an arbitrary one: he could have been nice to every one, and given everybody a good time, but has reserved that for his selected favourites, and written off the rest.

If we avoid the second mistake, that of construing salvation as some external state of physical affairs, we avoid the first one also. For love, if it is to be love, must be freely given: else, whatever else it is, it is not love. If to be loved by God is the *summum bonum*, then at once it follows that we cannot have or acquire a right to be loved, we cannot merit it or earn it, for if we could, it would not be love. What then can we do? Is there nothing we can do? God simply loves us, full stop? We are merely the passive recipients of his irresistible good will? Such a view has been held, but accords ill with our relationship with God being a personal one. For personal relations are two-way. Without some reciprocity on our part, however finite and feeble in the face of God's infinitude, we could not talk of there being personal relations. Nor is there any need for us to say that there is nothing we can do if we value God's love. All we have shown is that we cannot manipulate God into loving us, nor lay him under an obligation to do so. The man who is wooing a woman can neither manipulate her into loving him, nor claim that she is, or would be if he performed certain feats, under an obligation to love him: but there are many things he still can do; things which are pleasing to her, things which will show her his ardent devotion. So too, though differently, with God. We cannot manipulate, we cannot claim rights, but we can do those things that we believe will please him, we can show our devotion to him in our actions as well as in our thoughts.

St Paul's antithesis between justification by faith and justification by works expresses the truth that salvation—being in the love of God—depends on one's attitude of mind, and is not a matter of technique or legal claims. It can be secured only by a whole-hearted approach, in contradistinction to states of affairs in the natural world which can be brought about, irrespective of our attitude, so long as we observe the laws of nature; and in contradistinction to legal rights which can be secured and exercised as much by a bad man as by a good. The antithesis is easily misconstrued. 'Faith' is thought to exclude 'works', and *vice versa*. But St Paul did not mean to say that 'good works' were not pleasing to God. What he was castigating was not the doing of good works or the keeping of the Law, but the attitude of mind which relied on good works done or legal provisions kept to secure what could only be secured by a whole-hearted commitment. The antithesis is between a whole-hearted commitment to God—*pistis eis Christon Iesoun*—and an attempt to deal with God at a distance, keeping him at arm's length while using him for one's own ends. This was the Pharisees' failing. Their overt behaviour conformed to the pattern required, but inwardly their attitude was still that of getting the best for number one. They kept the Law, but thought in terms of solicitors' letters to God, claiming his love as a right.

It is a condition of our being autonomous independent self-conscious centres of action that we can in general manage with a less than whole-hearted response. If the aircraftsman could not, in general, achieve his mundane purposes in his ordinary clothes, he would not have any independent mastery over nature, but would be at best simply a vessel of the divine purpose, effective when co-operating with it, but impotent to achieve anything if his attitude was wrong. Only by shielding men's inmost thoughts from the world, and by making the actual attitude of mind be causally irrelevant, and by allowing an ill will to be as effective as a good will, so long as the effective means were adopted—only so could God make men independent enough to be his children and to be able to bestow, or not to bestow, a love that was worth the having. A certain privacy of intent is a necessary condition of being an independent agent. But autonomy breeds separation and alienation. Man must be a manipulator or impotent. But man the mere manipulator is lonely. 'Glory to Man in the Highest, for he is the Master of things', sang Swinburne, but the mere mastery of things does not make a man glorious, because it leaves him—his will, the essential him—opaque. We know what he does, but we cannot get to know him as he is, if he is a manipulator only. We cannot get through to him, and he cannot get through to us, unless each abandons his solipsistic privacy, and reveals himself in a personal relation. But to do this is to abandon one's privilege as a manipulator: each must treat the other not merely as a means, but also as an end in himself. In so doing, each loses the sense of being alien and utterly separate from the other, and in the fusion of good will they achieve a common sentiment and understanding which transcends the logical loneliness of their separate egocentric predicaments.

The Fall and the Redemption are two stages in man's pilgrimage into freedom and fulfilment. If man is to be free, he must have the power of saying No, the ability to choose ends other than those God would have him seek, and he must have also the power to pursue these ends effectively. But if he is to find fulfilment in life he must be able to find ends worth pursuing for their own sake, not simply because he happens to choose them; and the ends which are most worth pursuing are persons. God is a person, and our relationship with him is to be construed by analogy with our relations with human beings. But we cannot keep ourselves up to the standard of perfection required. With fallible and fickle human beings we are kept on our best behaviour by the realization that if we let our guard slip (and even if we do not), they may withdraw their favour. Therefore we must do our best. And with finite human beings, it is always possible that they will not realize how much less than whole-hearted we are: therefore our actual performance can be good enough for them. But with God we easily lack the incentive: we know that he is not arbitrary, and are inclined to trade on it. And any actual performance—*erga* works—less than a whole hearted acceptance of his love, and total commitment to him, *pistis*, is too little. Our second best is not enough. But we keep on trying to delude ourselves that it is; keep on trying to keep God at a distance, while enjoying his presence and his company. We, natural men that we are, want God to be a possession, which we can manipulate, not a person. Like the Pharisees. But to want that is to want not to be a person oneself; it is to want to be a whited sepulchre, dead, under the Law, not alive in Christ.

We are always, because we are fallible, liable to harden our hearts and become Pharisees: but there is no fulfilment, no satisfaction in that sort of life, and we are constantly needing to break out of it and to be renewed as persons. This is what it is to be a person. This is what it is to be alive.

3 GRACE

When a Christian is asked to explain his actions he gives reasons; and if questioned further, gives further, deeper reasons. If the questions are pressed to the limit, he will account for his actions not as dictated by an impersonal moral law nor as being simply the outcome of an arbitrary choice, but as spelling out his love of God. And if pressed further, why he does, or why he should, love God, he replies that we love God, because he first loved us. And if he is then pressed further why God does, or why he should, love him, he has no further answer to offer. 'He just does', he says; 'no reason why he should—certainly not for any merit of mine—, but nevertheless he does; out of the overflowing goodness of his heart, he has been pleased to lavish on me the fulness of his love.'

This is grace, the unmerited favour shown by God towards a man, the ultimate spring of action in a Christian man. We can take it, as I have taken it, as the ultimate reason; we can also consider it as answering a question of psychology, how a less-than-perfect man came to be able to act in the way in which, admittedly, a perfectly rational agent would act. This was the form in which the grace of God was known in the New Testament. It was not so much that the fact of being loved by God afforded the apostles a good reason for loving God in return, as that the realization of being loved by God made them able to overcome all their natural fears and weaknesses. Pentecost was, if you will forgive the metaphor, the engagement party of the Church and the Holy Ghost, when the saints walked on air and found all things were possible to them whom God had so greatly loved. Later, when the effervescence had subsided, and perhaps particularly with St Paul, it was a sense of divine commission that carried Christians through tribulations and temptation. Again the parallel holds with ordinary life: it is easier to get up early in the morning if one has been entrusted with an important task; the soldier-boy carrying a special message from the commander-in-chief draws from this commission new courage, new strength, new resource; knowing that he is the authorized representative of the Queen, the ambassador acquires an authority of demeanour, and can stand his ground in the face of hostility and abuse. And so the members of the apostolic Church, even after the honeymoon was over, retained the sense of privilege, in being the chosen instruments of God, in being trusted to help carry out his purposes here on earth. And the knowledge of having been chosen and of being trusted gave Christians then, as it gives bishops priests and laymen now, a feeling of confidence, a sense of purpose and drive, resolution and initiative. There is nothing mysterious about the grace of Orders: it operates in a perfectly straightforward fashion; to know that one is loved and that one has been selected for a special task is a factor that, as a matter of simple human psychology, often enables a man to achieve unity of purpose and to overcome all manner of difficulties, both internal and external. Only, how much more when it is by God that one is loved and has been chosen.

The concept of grace can thus be taken in two ways. It can be taken as playing a logical part when we give a rationale of our actions: or it can be taken as a psychological concept figuring in an explanation of our actions in causal terms. In the one case it is God's love towards us that is the ultimate ground for our acting after the example of Christ: in the other it is our realization of God's love towards us that is the most important factor in bringing it about that we act after the example of Christ. These two ways are so closely related as to make it unnecessary to distinguish them, except in order to ward off confusions that may arise when thinkers whose piety outruns their acuteness begin to reflect on their springs of action. In either way of taking the concept, we are assigning the ultimate responsibility for the Christian man's Christian actions to God. For responsibility is answerability, and the question a man has to answer is the question 'Why did you do it?' and to this question the Christian man answering for his Christian actions must ultimately give as his answer the love of God, unmerited and undeserved, given not as of right but simply by God's favour. God is the initiator, the *arche tou kinein*, the unmoved mover; and therefore to God, not to the individual Christian, is to be ascribed the merit, the honour, the glory and the praise.

If we do not sufficiently distinguish the two roles of the concept of grace, we may transfer the rational necessity that inheres in right actions to a psychological account in which necessity is entirely incompatible with an action's being an action, either right or wrong, at all. Whenever we are pressed to the limit to say why we did an action, our account, if satisfactory, must show why, in view of the circumstances known to us at the time, we had to act as we did. A rational man, when he has given all the answers he can give, must be able then to say, 'So you see: here stood I: I could no other'. This seems to me, though not to many contemporary philosophers, a perfectly proper sense of the modal words 'had to' 'could' 'necessity'. Not a logical necessity, nor a physical necessity, nor always a moral necessity, but what, for want of a better term, I shall call a rational necessity. It seems to me that we do use modal concepts in some such loosely defined way, and that it is implicit in our idea of reasonable argument that we should be able to use them so. But, of course, however cogent or compelling or coercive a rational agent finds some argument, he is not compelled to act on them in the way that a prisoner may be compelled to act on his gaoler's instructions, nor is he subject to the sort of inner compulsion that compels a kleptomaniac to steal.

The concept of necessity is not only systematically ambiguous, but parallels the concept of explanation in its ambiguities. Every explanation, if sufficiently completed, will lead to the conclusion that it had to be so, it could not have been otherwise. The necessities and impossibilities thus revealed obtain their colouring from the explanations leading up to them, and as there are different types of explanation, so there are different types of necessity and impossibility; and thus the same course of action will appear necessary or not necessary according to the type of explanation the speaker has in mind; and therefore the concept of grace, capable as it is of playing different roles in different types of explanation is peculiarly liable to generate confusion. And while it is fairly easy to see how the language of rational necessity may be extended to confer a spurious causal or psychological necessity on right actions, it is less easy to give any account in causal or psychological terms that is philosophically adequate. Let me only make two points: first that any causal or psychological explanation of human actions runs into difficulty because it must either appear incomplete or else leave no room for free rational choice, which is the hallmark of an action's being an action; the difficulty here is not one peculiar to grace in its original sense, though it has ensnared those who have sought an extended use of the concept. Secondly, the question that seeks a psychological explanation in terms of grace, is not 'Why did you do it?' but 'How were you able to do it?'. The characteristic of Christians in the apostolic age which excited most comment and admiration among pagans was not the high standard of ethical aspiration they set themselves—many pagans did so almost as much—but their ability to achieve so much. Many Pharisees had standards every bit as exacting as those of St Paul; but who among them was able to labour so abundantly, in journeyings often, in tribulations often, beset by perils without and weakness within? It was this power to carry on and succeed that impressed both those who witnessed it and those who experienced it, and was by Christians attributed to God under the name of grace. But no explaining how a man is able to do something should be taken for an explanation of why he must. What is to be explained is that a man *can* do something, and no explanation of that can be charged with determinist menace.

Yet it remains very easy to confuse the proposition that one can succeed with the proposition that one cannot fail. 'If God be for us, who can be against us?' we ask, and do not pause to consider the case when we are not for God, so that God cannot be, in a simple and uncomplicated way, for us. The ability that the knowledge of God's love towards him gives the Christian becomes a power, God's power, God's irresistible power, and the stage is all set for Pelagius' protest.

We may see in this transition not only the shift that often occurs in the history of ideas, but the resurgence of the old Adam in the Christian mind. The 'I, yet not I' of St Paul was meant as the negation of ego-centricity: and in St Paul's mouth it was—so far as it is given to any fallen man to be utterly unselfish. But humility easily becomes the occasion of new forms of pride, and 'I, yet not I' can become a far more terrible boast than simple, godless conceit. To be entirely certain that one is the chosen instrument of God's will makes for great moral fervour and effectiveness, but the partnership between God and oneself can be readily misconstrued, and the belief that God is on one's side can easily degenerate into the assumption of a celestial underwriting of all one's actions, that God is in one's pocket. But if it is power that is the mark of grace, there is not much to choose between the two beliefs on the score of effectiveness. Cromwell and Gladstone were as powerful as St Paul. If once we commend Christianity on the grounds that it makes for effective personalities, the type of God we had imagined would prove a useful servant turns out to be an annihilating master. The price of power is to purport to be a puppet.

Pelagius understood about freedom, and the non-necessity, in the relevant sense, of our loving God in response to his love for us; but failed, in our eyes, to appreciate the importance of the antecedence of God's love for us, and that it was this that distinguished Christianity from other religions. Pelagianism was like humanism, a religion of good men who had decided to lead the moral life. It has no sense of the *privilege* that the Christian feels, when he realizes that God loves him, and *therefore*, we should say, none of the power and none of the humility of the Christian. We are tempted to make too much of the power, and to neglect the sense of privilege that gives it, and the humility which comes equally with it. It is a strong point in apologetics that Christianity is effective in redeeming bad men, where Pelagianism and humanism have nothing to say except to men who have already decided to be good; they can give no reason why one should try to be good, no help in making the effort. But it is not simply the Salvation Army aspect of Christianity which distinguishes it from other religions: it is, rather, the being-loved-ness; and the manifestation of this should be much more humility than power. Lack of pretension, lack of pride induced by the knowledge that one is loved by God, in much the same way as they are induced by the knowledge that one is loved by a person—these are the crucial characteristics of the Christian. Just as the ordinary barriers men erect around themselves and the ordinary images they seek to project of themselves, are broken down in personal relationships, so, only much more so, the love of God gets through to people and enables them to be honest with themselves, to be authentic, to be real, to be themselves. This may make some men more effective, by freeing them from the crippling illusions about themselves or by giving them a singleness of purpose previously lacking; but when a person is being himself, and not thinking of himself more highly than he ought, it is his humility rather than his effectiveness that we chiefly note.

4 PROVIDENCE

The concept of providence is a negative concept. When we talk about providence we mean in short how God is working his purposes out apart from our own, perhaps puny, efforts. I do not ascribe it to providence, though I may ascribe it to grace, when, after a great deal of hard lobbying, I manage to obtain planning permission for the building of a church hall. It is when God seems to be furthering his purposes, either for me individually or for mankind as a whole, but not through me, and often in spite of my non-co-operation, that I want to talk of providence. We suspect some providential ordering of events when our own plans, retrospectively realized to have been wrong plans, are frustrated, or when our good plans are brought to a good success not because we were in a position to bring them through, but because a happy conjunction of circumstances makes good our own deficiencies. A don may come to regard it as providential that he did not get a Fellowship in a particular college which at the time he had very much wanted to get; many people regard it as providential that Hitler, according to one account, held back his panzers from en-circling the British Expeditionary Force in May 1940; and that the weather was fair and calm during the evacuation of Dunkirk.

There are some sorts of providence about which there are no philosophical difficulties—God's general providence in creating a universe which is an instantiation of intelligible principles, in sending us rain in due season and in making the earth fruitful. This I shall not discuss. I shall discuss, rather, the sort of Providence which raises difficulties.

There seem to be three difficulties: first the plausible sugges-tion that we invent providence in retrospect; providence lies in the eye of the beholder: second the collision between God's ordering things and man's free-will; how could God have made Hitler do such a silly thing as to hold back his panzers: third whether it is consonant with the dignity of God to try and fix things for the benefit of me, who am after all only one pebble on a very large beach.

The suggestion that we invent providence in retrospect is very plausible. We read into events a pattern that is not there. Since the specification of the pattern is very imprecise, it is not too difficult to find in most courses of events some pattern that can be subsumed under the specification. Moreover, there is a further reason why we should find this easy: in our interpretations of our own individual histories we are all Whigs; we think that what is now is what ought to be, and that we can properly construe the past as leading up to, and being intended to lead up to, the present. The causal pattern that we can quite properly find in past events and which provides a historical explanation of the present state of affairs, thus becomes a teleological explanation, showing how the course of events in time past was intended to bring us to our present state. And since we are never wholly masters of our destiny, it is tempting to see not only in our decisions but in all the efficacious factors which were outside our control the same great design, shaping our lives and guiding us to where we ought to be. And this, the sceptic will say, is all an illusion.

How can this objection be answered? I do not think it can, at least not on the level at which it is made. People are not convinced of the existence of God as a necessary inference to be drawn from the manifest workings of providence. It is ony if one already believes in the existence of a personal God, involved in this world, and concerned to work out his purposes in the course of history that we wonder how this might be possible. For any one convinced of the non-existence of God, no argument from providence can be drawn; or rather, the accusation of Whiggery is a complete counter—though later, I shall hope to show, the Whig argument can be turned inside out.

The difficulty about human freedom divides into two. One might take freedom in a very strong sense, where it would be impossible for a man to act freely and at the same time help to carry out a divine plan, except by coincidence. I see no force in this contention. It seems to me perfectly possible for God to act through the actions of free men freely co-operating with him—after all, it is possible even for men to do as much. In the case of God's calling a man directly, there seems to me no derogation from his freedom if he answers. Ananias' arrival at Saul's lodging place was providential for Saul; but Ananias acted quite freely, if somewhat unwillingly, in going to see him. The cases where God does not deal with men by direct communication are less easy—would it be consonant with God's frankness to 'get' Hitler to hold back his divisions at Boulogne? About this let me say for the moment only that it concerns God's frankness not man's freedom. Hitler was perfectly free to let his panzers press on, even if he decided otherwise, and even if his wrong decision issued from his own vanity and pride. We may demand that God should not make use of our weaknesses to achieve his ends, though I am not sure how far we are entitled to make this demand: but we cannot complain that we were unfree, when the choices we make through pride turn out to frustrate the plans which we in pride set up in opposition to God's will.

There remains, however, a serious difficulty about freedom and providence. If men really are free, then it is always possible that they will take a series of decisions which will effectively frustrate what, so far as we had been able to make it out, had been God's intended plan. And, again so far as we can make out these things, it seems that this often actually happens. It is not an answer to this to say *simply* (and often complacently) that whatever disasters befall us, we always can turn them to good account. The uses of adversity may be sweet, but if my belief that God has a plan for me which I ought to do my best to carry out, is to have any muscle in it, it must not mean merely that whatever happens is God's will. If I am to bend my efforts to fulfil God's will, then I must believe that some states of affairs rather than others are what God wants to come about. But if God's designs are thus non-vacuous for me, they are vulnerable towards others. For many of the things I can try to bring about in accordance with what I take to be God's will, can be brought to naught by the non-co-operation of others; and others, as we all know to our cost, often will not co-operate. And so God's plans it seems are either vacuous or else the victim of every bloodyminded man, and ineffective.

I think the latter horn of the dilemma is the cross on which God has chosen to be impaled. God's designs for the world cannot be capable of a vacuous fulfilment, or he would be a Lucretian or deistic deity, not seriously concerned with the affairs of this world, not a God of love. It is the corollary of caring, that one should be vulnerable, and a God who cares infinitely will be infinitely vulnerable. Thus far, on this score there need be no difficulty: we view the course of history as a continuing crucifixion, the price of loving people who are free not to love in

29

return. The difficulty comes when we consider not the readiness of God to suffer but the effectiveness of his will. What is the analogue of the resurrection? How are God's designs vindicated if they are always to be vulnerable to our non-co-operation? The answer, I think, lies in the infinitude of God, and his infinite resource. One plan may fail, but there are always others. As fast as we torpedo his best designs for us, he produces out of his agonized reappraisal a second best. It is the same as with human plans. When we fail to bring them off, we modify them. The fact that our plans are flexible, and have to be continually reviewed and altered in the light of circumstances, does not make them vacuous, or mean that whatever the outcome is, it will count as the implementation of a plan. Far less so with God. Whatever the situation, there are some things he would rather have us do than other things; and in so far as we do them, we are fulfilling *a* plan he has for us; in so far as we do not, we shall be bringing about a situation, undesired if not always unforeseen, which will call for new remedies of its own, new remedies which will themselves call once again for our co-operation if they are to be carried out.

It is an error to talk about God's blueprint for the world. Any single design so detailed and exact as a blueprint must be Procrustean. If we are to admit human freedom, then we must either understand by design only the barest outline, so that no non-co-operation on the part of any finite creature could make a significant difference to it, or else, as I have been doing, replace the singular by a plural, and allow that an infinite God has an infinite set of blueprints, so that whatever situation emerges as a result of men's folly or bloodymindedness, there is a definite course of action that God would have us take.

The conflict between freedom and providence has been eased, not solved. We have seen how providence can be consistent with freedom, just as grace can. If men will co-operate, their co-operation is free, although their actions can properly be ascribed to God's design: and if they will not, then God is prepared to take the knock and think afresh. But the common notion of providence is not simply that of God's working his purposes out through the willing co-operation of his creatures, but is in large measure a notion of God's getting his own way in spite of our own wishes to the contrary. It was this that gave the Old Testament writers their sense of the inexorability of God; and we still are inclined to look for poetic justice in the course of human affairs, and to believe that the mills of God can grind smaller than any human devices. And here the conflict with freedom seems much more acute. It was no willing co-operation on Hitler's part that led him to halt his panzers; but if God made him do it willy-nilly, surely this is an infringement of freedom. Did God make Hitler mad in order to destroy him?

This rhetorical question half suggests its own answer. God did not make Hitler mad, but Hitler made himself mad, through his own overwhelming pride. God's influence is to be seen not in an arbitrary interference with Hitler's free-will, but in having made men as he has made them, with the grain of human nature such that God's purposes tend to be fulfilled, and that those who would frustrate him are themselves frustrated. Whether or not Hitler had intervened before Dunkirk, he was making himself into the person who would gratuitously invade Russia, take on America, sacrifice one army at Stalingrad and another in Tunisia. The sin of pride becomes the disease of megalomania: and the disease of megalomania sooner or later precludes the recognition of what things are and are not possible in nature, which is the foundation of all effective action. We may properly attribute to God the particular events which are instances of this principle: but this need not be because God interfered. God always can interfere: he may have sent lying prophets to mislead as he did to mislead Ahab; but perhaps in neither case was it necessary for God to intervene. Hitler and Ahab both showed themselves perfectly capable of compassing their own destruction; in particular, because both of them were determined to hear only what they wanted to hear they made sure that their information would be fashioned to fit their fads rather than the facts.

Men being what they are, certain themes will recur time and time again in the course of history. High ideals will be insidiously corrupted by the self-love of those who profess them: but the power of self-love will always be fragmented and variable, because every self-lover will be loving a different self, and any coincidence of interest will be only transient. Original sin, which trips us up when we aim to be gods, prevents us in even greater measure from being very effective in the production of evil. Private vices often become public virtues, in history as well as political economy, not because God intervenes to nullify the consequences of men's ill-intentioned acts, but because this is the natural outcome of the interplay of conflicting interests. Poetic justice will often be done, because men, being what they are, distrust the untrustworthy, fear or hate those who hurt them, occasionally even requite well-doing with well-doing. It is not an exact justice, nor is it a divine justice—it would be counter to God's intention of creating us free agents, if he were to attach to each one of our doings an exactly proportioned reward or penalty; but it is possible to regard this rough justice as a divine retribution, in that it was God who created us as we are, and that if he had created us differently—if, for example, we did not object to being deceived, or if our invariable response to force was a cowering adulation, if we always kissed the hand that hit us—then the course of history would be very different, and nobody would ever be tempted to see moral principles at work in it. As it is, although we are free to act as we please, and can hope to escape the consequences of our actions and quite often do, there is nevertheless built into the fabric of social existence a certain pressure towards some degree of right doing, and people who act against the grain of human nature are apt to find their purposes frustrated in ways they never anticipated, even though in retrospect we feel that it was only to be expected that their evil enterprises should fail in the way they did. The tide of human affairs is a school of virtue, though not a nursery. Just as the material world is one which man can come to understand and to control, although remaining one in which he can suffer grievous hurt, often undeserved, so social existence in company with his fellow men is the way in which the best in man is educated, though without his being insulated in any way from the most terrible disasters. And just as we may see the whole natural order as the activity, though not the intervention, of God, so we may see our Creator at work also in the ordinary course of the historical process.

I want to turn the Whig argument inside out. The fact that people can read a providential design into their own personal histories does not show that the design is illusory, but witnesses rather to something special about them, something God has given them. In fact three things. First, the very argument used against the Whig interpretation cuts two ways. For it will only work because men are capable of working out their own salvation. The reason why we think our present situation is the right one is because, when we previously thought that a particular course of action was the right one to take, we were able to take it; or that a particular situation was the one we ought to bring about, we were able—to some extent—to bring it about. But this power of making the best of our circumstances is itself providential. The anti-Whig argument itself witnesses to the rationality of man, the way in which men are made in the image of God.

Secondly, a point which now needs little further argument, the same graining of human nature which makes God's purposes work out in spite of men's non co-operation, make each man's individual experience in life into a tutorial in morality. We learn by our failures; and can quite properly see in them in retrospect the needful conditions of our subsequent successes. This is what I meant when I said that people might be persuaded, though they could not be convinced, by their own experience in life. They may keep coming up against something other than themselves making for good; and may come to recognize it, or rather him, as such. It was hard, they found, to kick against the pricks.

The third reason for discerning the activity of God in ordinary historical events arises not from their tendency to conspire together for good, but from our ability to turn them to good effect. The facile optimism that holds that out of evil good will always come is false: but it remains the case that out of evil good always can come, if we so choose, thanks to the power, given to us by God through Christ's suffering on the cross, to consecrate suffering and transform disaster into triumph. Things do not always turn out for the best. There are real disasters. God's plans for us, like our own plans for ourselves, are always liable to be frustrated by our own failures and the evil-doing of others. But we can turn things, whatever they happen to be, to the best, because, God being infinite, there is not just one best, which if frustrated we can never hope to recapture or recreate, but an infinity of bests, so that the very loss of one makes possible the achievement of another. It is our life to make what we can of circumstances, and we always can make something creative of them, although we do not always do so, and although it is much more difficult to do so in some cases than in others. But *chalepa ta kala*, and the greatest triumphs are those that overcome the greatest obstacles, and we do not expect it always to be easy going, nor would we like it if it was.

As we look back on our lives, we see external circumstances as the context in which they were lived and the necessary condition of our having made whatever we did make of them. Christians ascribe such success as they make of their lives to God, and are therefore inclined to describe those conditions of their success that are external to themselves as being the activity of God, whereby he enabled their lives to be brought to a good success. Such a description is right, in that God is the creator of all things, including the circumstances in which we find ourselves and God is responsible for the success we are able to make of our lives; but the description can mislead, for it suggests that God 'fixed' external circumstances in order to set the stage for us to play out our life-drama on; whereas God's goodness towards any one of us on this score lies not in his having arranged the world around to suit him, making it just difficult enough to try him but not to break him, but rather in his having enabled him to transmute, if only by accepting and suffering them, all the trials of this life into something glorious. We are right to ascribe this to God: but wrong to suggest that God's activity here is taking the form of a special intervention in order to rig the course of events for the benefit of some persons rather than others.

5   ROGATIONTIDE QUERIES

Christians have always felt some hesitation in asking God to do things. In spite of Christ's clear injunction to the contrary, they have felt that they ought not to bother God with their prayers, because to do so seems to cast aspersions on his wisdom and providence. In A.D. 233 Ambrose, a friend of Origen, put the matter succinctly thus, 'First: if God knows the future before-hand, and it must come to pass, prayer is vain. Secondly: if all things happen according to the will of God, and if what is willed by him is fixed, and nothing of what he wills can be changed, prayer is vain'.[1]

The first difficulty is not specifically about prayer. It is the difficulty of theological determinism, which arises for any one who affirms the existence of an omniscient God. Future events 'have been determined by necessity because God, who knows the future beforehand, cannot lie'.[2] If God knew for certain yesterday what I shall do tomorrow, then it is not possible today that I shall not do it.

The traditional answer to this problem has been to claim that my will is nonetheless free, because God's foreknowledge is not a *cause* of the predicted action's taking place, and that therefore God is not responsible, but man, who does cause it.

> They, therefore, as to right belonged,
> So were created, nor can justly accuse
> Their Maker, or their making, or their fate;
> As if predestination overruled
> Their will, disposed by absolute decree
> Or high foreknowledge; they themselves decreed
> Their own revolt, not I: if I foreknew,
> *Foreknowledge had no influence on their fault,*
> Which had no less proved certain unforeknown.[3]

---

[1] Origen, *De Oratione*, V. 6. translation in J. E. L. Oulton and H. Chadwick, *Alexandrian Christianity*, Library of Christian Classics, vol. II (London 1954), p. 250; see also pp. 180–2.
[2] Id. ibid. p. 252.
[3] J. Milton, *Paradise Lost*, III, ll. 111–119; my italics.

This answer cannot be sustained. Even though God had not himself caused our actions, it would not make them any the more free, if he nonetheless knew infallibly what it was we were going to do. God might not have caused our actions, but neither should we have caused them, if they could have been predicted long before we had decided to do them, perhaps even long before we were born.

But perhaps they could not have been predicted, not even by God. Nor, according to some philosophers, need this be any derogation from God's omniscience. God knows all things, all things that can be known. But future events, apart from those that are 'already present in their causes', are not knowable, and therefore cannot be known even by God. We do not regard it as any limitation of God's omniscience that he cannot know that two and two make five; neither should we think it at all strange that he cannot know what I am going to do in advance of my deciding what to do, since in that case too there is nothing for God to know, and so no possible criticism of him for not knowing it.

Knowledge is not like sight, nor is time like space. We are too ready to follow Boethius, and think of God's omniscience as a form of all-seeingness, and remote stretches of the future like remote regions of space, which, however inaccessible to us, would be immediately accessible to the infinite mind of an omnipresent Deity. But the logic of knowledge is more complicated than that of sight, and if we take time seriously at all, it becomes problematic whether future contingent propositions can, in general, be knowable, or, indeed, can even be said to be true or false.

Quite apart from these logical and conceptual difficulties, we may also ease the problem of God's foreknowledge by drawing a parallel between his omniscience and his omnipotence. Although God is able to do all things, we do not think he does do all things. Not only do we often ascribe events to human agencies or natural causes rather than to divine action, but we allow that some things happen against God's will. Although he could intervene to prevent the plans of the wicked from coming to fruition, often he does not. And the reason commonly given by theologians is that God often refrains from intervening in the world in order to preserve man's freedom of choice. He allows man to be independent and to make real choices which are really effective, in spite of the fact that they are often not the choices that God would have had us make, and in spite of the fact that they will often involve other men in un-deserved suffering. But if God is prepared to compromise his om-nipotence for the sake of human freedom, surely then he would be prepared to compromise his omniscience also. If he suffers his will to be confined, in order that his creatures may have room to make their own decisions, he must allow his understanding to be abridged, in order to allow men privacy to form their own plans for themselves.

It seems to me entirely unobjectionable that God should limit his infallible knowledge as he does his power, in order to let us be independent of him. Such a self-limitation would not be open to Leibniz' objection that it would make God 'like the God of the Socinians, who lives only from day to day'. For it limits only his infallible knowledge. God could still know us and predict our ac-tions in the way our friends do, without its constituting any threat to freedom. The Christian religion, with its emphasis on the humanity of God, must ascribe to him all human modes of knowledge, as well as the more absolute ones of theism generally. Fallible foreknowledge is enough to enable God not to live only from day to day, but to foresee the likely course of events and to take such actions, consistent with human freedom, as will work out for the best in the context of those decisions men are likely to take.

The second difficulty concerns the perfection not of God's knowledge but of his plans. He, surely, already knows what is best for us, and will have already disposed all things for the best. If what we ask for is for the best, God will bring it about, whether we ask for it or not; if what we ask for is not for the best, then God will not do what we want, even though we ask him to. So either way, prayer is ineffective.

One move is to concede that prayer is ineffective, but deny that it is irrelevant. By asking God to do things, we make his actions our own. We identify our wills with his will, and take responsibili-ty for the future course of events in the only way that is open to finite, limited, men. Besides, God likes to be asked, even if, like parents making plans for their children, he will make and carry out his plans for our sakes even in the absence of any specific requests.

Both these contentions have force, but neither can be a com-plete answer. Prayer should not be solely petitionary. We ought not only to ask God for the things we want, but equally to ask God what thing we ought to want. We should seek a union of wills: not simply by telling God what we want, but by letting him tell us what he wants. In so far as we say, and really mean it, 'Yet not as I will, but as thou wilt', our prayer ceases to be petitionary and becomes conversational. And this is, at least within limits, a gain. So too, it is a gain to say 'Give us this day our daily bread', and thereby make the future provision of our needs, which, for us at least, whether we say our prayers or not, is pretty well secure, a gift, freely given and gratefully received, rather than a bare, un-valued result of our own contriving. God sends the rain to the just and the unjust: but to the just who has asked for it, it comes as a token of God's goodness, whereas to the unjust, who never says 'Please' and never says 'Thank you' it is a mere climatic condition, without significance and without being an occasion for gratitude; and the unjust's life is thereby poorer and drearier.

Nevertheless these do not constitute a complete answer. Although many people are wrong in thinking of prayer as being always petitionary, it is equally distorting to make out petitionary prayer as being necessarily ineffective. Christ would have been misleading his disciples when he said 'Whatsoever ye shall ask of the Father in my name, he shall give it you' (John 15. 16), if he sup-pressed a further conditional clause, 'always provided that it was what he was going to do anyhow'. A language without an im-perative mood is radically defective, and imperatives are meant to be acted on. If we are to be able to communicate with God, we must be able to communicate our pleas as well as listen to his call: and these pleas cannot all be totally ineffective. If God is a person who can hear our prayers, we, limited mortal men, shall ask God to do things for us, things which we want, not necessarily things that he wants. Christ's rider, 'Nevertheless, not as I will, but as thou wilt' is typically untypical. Nobody but he could say it and mean it all the time; few can say it with complete sincerity at any time. Most people would far rather that God should do what they want than that he should do what he wants. The furthest that many can go, is to accept God's No with resignation. It is not in our nature to want to have our wants denied.

The theologians' objections to allowing that God might be moved by prayer to alter the course of events are not as weighty as they make out. The argument from changelessness is totally mis-conceived. For change, like sameness and difference, is an incomplete concept: we always need to specify with respect to what something has changed, or is the same as or is different from some other thing. God is changeless in some respects—in his goodness and his love and his faithfulness: but he changes in other respects—at one time the Father was going to send his Son into the world, at another time he was communing with him in the wilderness, and now he has raised him from the dead. Indeed, if God could not change in any respect, he would not be a person at all, since personality implies consciousness and consciousness implies change.

The straight argument from changelessness is without merit, although hallowed by tradition. More weighty is the argument that for God to have second thoughts about what he was going to do either implies that the first thoughts were not the best possible ones or else is a change for the worse. Behind this argument lies the assumption, natural for monotheism, that there is only one best plan, so that if everything is for the best, it is completely determinate. But the superlative does not logically imply uniqueness, and Christianity, although monotheistic, is not, *pace* St Augustine, totally theocentric. God has given men free-will, and made them independent originators of action. His providence therefore is vulnerable to men's independent action. Whatever harmony he may have hoped for, some man somewhere at some time may choose to strike a discordant note. Therefore in giving men free-will God has already forgone the absolute monolithic excellence that a solipsistic monad might have managed. God's plan for the future must be like that of the Persian rugmakers, who let their children help them. In each family the children work at one end of the rug, the father at the other. The children fail to carry out their father's instructions exactly, but so great is their father's skill, that he adapts his design at his end to take in each error at the children's end, and work it into a new, constantly adapted, pattern. So too, God. He does not, cannot, have one single plan for the world, from which we, by our errors, ignorances, and sins, are ever further departing. His plans are for the future only, taking into account what the present has turned out to be; and when, as often, we fail to do what he had it in mind for us to do, God does not relapse into the counterfactual optative mood, but goes on from where we have already landed ourselves. God does not have just one plan for the world, but an infinity of plans, and with the changing course of events selects those that are applicable to the actual circumstances that obtain.

We are compelled thus far to compromise the uniqueness of God's Providence simply in view of man's free-will. But we need to go even further if we ascribe to men some independent value as well as a capacity for independent action. For then not only may their actions alter the context in which God has to plan, but their desires will affect the scale of values according to which God will judge one plan to be better than another. For we are his children, not merely his recalcitrant sheep. Like a shepherd, God has to adjust his actions and plans to our wanderings and strayings, but far more than this, like a father, he takes into account our own views and inclinations. We are not only, though within limits, the originators of action, but also, though within limits, the origin of values. Just because a child values a woolly animal, it is valuable; just because her beau admired her dress, it is precious; so too, our mere wanting something may make it precious in the sight of God. This is not to say that anything we want we ought to get. Many of our desires are undesirable, and often the answer to our petitions must be No. But even though they must often be denied, they are not to be ignored. The mere fact that we want something is a reason, although not a conclusive reason, for God giving it us.

Two consequences follow: one for our view of God, the other for our practice of prayer. God is a deeply compromised God. By creating us and the world he has abdicated not merely absolute sway over the course of events but also absolute sway over the scale of values. In giving man free-will, the Creator had brought Christ's words 'Nevertheless, not as I will, but as thou wilt' into effect; and in hearkening to man's prayers, God makes the further concession 'Nevertheless, not as I would, but as thou wouldest'. Yet these concessions do not derogate from the majesty and magnificence of God. They are the concessions not of weakness but of strength. They are not forced on God by the recalcitrance of Platonic matter or the machinations of a Zoroastrian evil spirit: they are the freely accepted limitations of non-solipsistic creative activity. If God makes anything other than himself, he thereby compromises his sole position as the only pebble on the beach. To create is to abrogate. It is not a mere external ordinance imposed by the mere whim of God that to follow him we must deny ourselves, but one flowing from the inner nature of God himself. It is part of the internal pattern, of creating *something other than*, working itself out in the Christian life. Our exemplar is not only a suffering God, but a compromised one, who revealed his nature in the stable as well as on the cross.

In our practice of prayer, we can revert to the untutored outlook of ordinary men. We can say 'Please God, let Wolverhampton Wolves win and bring me a fortune on the pools'. We do not have to gloss it, as Christ did, with a 'nevertheless', nor do we have to steel ourselves to the knowledge that it will not make any difference whether we ask or not, but if it does come off, it will be nicer if we have asked. Yet we should not revert simply to the unsophisticated view. The ordinary man is apt to make a magician of God. Some requests should not be made because the mere making of them evinces a certain disrespect. Others may be made, but must expect the answer No. Others again, if made, may be granted, but it might be better if they were not made and not granted. Our wanting something does give it some value in the eyes of God, but often our wanting is not all that it should be, and could, if only we would, be better directed. Our wants, although not totally depraved, are far from perfect. We can, and should, better our wants by coming to want the things that God wants us to want. And if we want to know what things they are, the best way of finding out is to ask God. And, therefore, questions, as well as requests, are appropriate prayers for Rogationtide.

6 THE ORIGIN OF SIN

Let me begin with a confession of unbelief. I do not believe that there ever was a person called Adam, or that he had a wife called Eve, or that a snake was able to talk with Eve and suggest that she and Adam should eat some apples. For the rest, I am open minded about the evolution of man. It might be that all men now living are descended from just one pair of parents, but the balance of probabilities is against it. It might be that our genetic make-up includes some morally lethal gene, which arose as a result of a single mutation at a past moment of time, but I am sceptical about this, and in any case it is an acquired characteristic that Adam is supposed to have handed down.

My unbelief is nothing peculiar. I do not think I know of any Christian who *really* takes Genesis 2 and 3 as a literal historical account of what actually happened, in the way our ancestors did, or in the way that we take the Acts of the Apostles, or a scholar takes Thucydides. Nevertheless, Christians do not disown Genesis entirely. They hedge. While conceding that Genesis is not literally true, they claim that it contains symbolic truth notwithstanding. So far, so good. But it will not do to rest content with symbolic truth, a concept too vague to convey much meaning. We want to know how the symbolic truth is to be expressed non-symbolically. By this I do not mean that a complete translation in non-symbolic terms must be possible—for then the symbolism would be altogether otiose; but only that a partial translation in literal terms must be possible—for otherwise there would be no contact between 'symbolic truth' and everyday truth, and the symbolic truth could be just the reverse of what it is claimed to be, without its making any difference to our ordinary lives.

The story of the Fall represents an important truth about human nature. It is not about Adam, but about Man: it describes not what he did, but what we are. It is saying something about all of us, not because we happen to be the descendants of a particular man and have inherited responsibility for his wrongdoing, but because we are men, and, being such, have certain capacities, propensities, and weaknesses. For we are what we are in virtue of our common humanity, not of our possession of a common ancestor.

Three features of what it is to be a man are represented by the Genesis myth. There is first an account of our moral and spiritual maturation from a state of innocence to a state of adult autonomy. Each man in his own life and his own time comes to a knowledge of good and evil. The child is not aware at first of the possibility of straying off the path laid down for him by parent or pastor; but a sophisticated French intellectual is agonizingly aware of the different possibilities that there are, and how that it is for him to decide between them, and for him alone. The depth of the realization of our freedom and responsibility varies. Few experience it as the Existentialists do. Sometimes whole societies remain in a sort of state of innocence. Greece in the fifth and fourth centuries B.C. was losing its innocence; sophists were beginning to question moral standards, and there was no longer an unthinking acceptance of ancestral traditions. For most of us the loss of innocence is a gradual process; we lose it, not, as Adam is said to have done, in one fell swoop, but little by little, as we come to shake off habit and instinct and realize that on some particular issue we can act otherwise than we have been accustomed to, and ask ourselves 'What then shall we do?' None of us retains his innocence completely; few lose it completely. Most of us are all too well aware of our capacity for acting contrary to some standards, but continue to find some other sorts of behaviour quite unthinkable. Some men retain their certainty about the standards they ought to live up to, and discover only their ability not to; others find little difficulty in living up to any standards they accept, but have great doubts about what standards, if any, they should adopt. In all, our experience of the loss of innocence is much varied, and the only universal features are that we always regret it, yet always seek it. We look back with certain nostalgia to the days when life was simpler and less complicated than it is now, and feel that those days were idyllic and free, whereas now and hereafter life is toilsome and careworn. Nevertheless, we cannot, and even if we could, would not, go back. We are impelled to seek the knowledge of good and evil, however much it may hurt us. It is part of our development to adulthood, part of our becoming rational agents.

If we are to be conscious of the responsibility of freedom, we must know that there is a difference between right and wrong. If it did not matter which way we made the choice, we need not worry how we made it. A simple toss of the coin would suffice. But it does matter, and we know it, and hence the burden of deciding. We are aware, as human beings, of there being differences which matter, where we are bound to select the things that fall on one side of some distinction, and reject those on the other. We must believe the true and deny the false, do the right and eschew the wrong, accept the reasonable and decline the unreasonable, prefer the beautiful and avoid the ugly. We are not always able to distinguish the right, but we sometimes can, and we believe there is distinction to be drawn even when we are not able to draw it ourselves. In brief, Man is a rational animal. Unlike inanimate objects, which merely react to reagents, and unlike the animal creation, which merely respond to stimuli, men can think and can make rational judgements. In this they are like God. Genesis says that God made man in his image and likeness. And it is this, Man's capacity for being reasonable and right, that is the second feature of humanity Genesis portrays.

The third feature of humanity portrayed by Genesis is our self-centredness. Concomitant with the power to choose is a propensity to choose for one's own sake, regardless of all other considerations. The natural answer to 'What shall I do?' is 'What I want'. Self-awareness leads to self-centredness; our conception of autonomous agents is of beings who can say 'I shall do', 'I do', or 'I have done', and this 'I' injects a permanent note of egocentricity into the whole system. In logic and metaphysics as well as in morals, Man is in an egocentric predicament. His language and his knowledge of the world are anchored in himself and his experience; and to give an account of his relations with the external world and his fellow men, which does justice both to his sense of being set apart from everything else and to that of being involved in a world outside himself, has been one of the prime tasks of philosophers through the ages. In morals the self-centredness of man is more pervasive, and concerns not only the philosophically minded but all of us. The Christian maintains that in an important sense, human nature cannot be altered, and is incurably selfish. Although, in another sense, human nature can be altered, and we can instil into children all sorts of desirable habits and practices, yet, the Christian maintains, the old Adam in us will sooner or later obtain the upper hand, and men will convert the system with all its manners or *mores* to their own selfish ends, no matter how altruistic the original plan was. The history of monasticism in the Middle Ages and the more secular Utopias since shows how over the generations noble ends give way to private interests. If people cannot compete for wealth, they compete for power, and if not for power, for glory. The forms of life may change, and human nature is enormously adaptable, but always there remains an innate urge to do well by Number One. And this is our real origin of sin.

The word 'sin' is a theological term to which different meanings have been attached by different people. Hence it has been a source of confusion in Christian thought. In common speech, sin is understood to be a definite breach of some moral or ritual code, a moral and theological equivalent of the secular crime; some theologians, however, understood sin far more as a matter of one's spiritual relationship with God; sin is to be alienated from God and cut off from him, and the forgiveness of sin is a reconciliation and at-onement with him. Both senses are important: but they are different.

As regards the former sense, the doctrine of original sin has often been interpreted so as to be perfectly meaningful and obviously false. It has been said that nobody can help committing sin, except by the special grace of God. But there have been highly respectable and moral men outside the Christian Church, who either have never heard of Christ, like Socrates and Cato, or have definitely denied him, like John Stuart Mill or T. H. Huxley. Such men cannot be accounted sinners in the ordinary, moralist sense. No doubt they committed their peccadilloes. But it would be a trivial thing if the doctrine of original sin meant only that we all have some lapses much the same way as even the best marksmen do not hit the bull's eye every time. The good life, in the pagan sense of the phrase, is within the reach of the non-Christian, unsatisfactory though from the Christian point of view such a life would be. If it is maintained that such lives are nevertheless the result of an unrecognized and unacknowledged grace, we cannot deny that this may be so, but must point out that then the doctrine is becoming almost vacuous. If we are prepared to posit grace wherever we find goodness, it will be true that there is no goodness without grace: but the doctrine does not come to much; it is consistent with any set of facts of our moral experience; some people ask for divine assistance and are conscious of receiving it;

but other people are held to have received it without either having asked for it or having experienced it unasked. If the pagan who does not know or denies God may be given grace nonetheless to lead a good (by pagan standards) life without having ever sought divine assistance, it seems hard to condemn the Pelagian for not teaching the necessity of seeking grace. If we confine ourselves to overt behaviour, conscious seeking of assistance and awareness of its reception, then we must say that men can be good without having asked for, or recieved, divine aid. The doctrine of original sin, interpreted, as it sometimes has been, as the negation of this, is just simply false. Counter-examples abound.

Although the doctrine of original sin interpreted in this stringent sense is plainly false, there is a truth about overt behaviour worth expressing. It is generally, although not universally, the case that people fail to lead good lives. Moral codes have a tendency to be converted to selfish ends. The counter-examples cited in the last paragraph are exceptions. The general run of unredeemed humanity is to selfish and sub-standard behaviour. Individuals and communities have a natural propensity towards wickedness, and history can be described as the record of the crimes, misfortunes, and follies of mankind. Humanists may beg to differ; but the Christian claims, and can do so with some justification, that men, far from being naturally good, are naturally bad. Only, he must allow that there are exceptions to this generalization. The doctrine of original sin taken as a universal statement about all non-Christian men is indeed false: but taken as a generalization about non-Christian by and large, it may well be true. Just as our other generalizations—Woman is fickle; Men are brutes—are meant to be interpreted as generalizations only and not as excluding exceptions entirely, and may well then be true, so the Christian insight that man is not naturally good is to be interpreted in a similar fashion.

The confusion of Christian theologians over the doctrine of original sin is only in part due to the different senses of the word 'sin'. The Christian is also tempted to affirm that nobody can be good without the aid of God, because he does not see why an unbeliever should live up to the standards required of him. The Christian has a *rationale* of morality. He can return an answer to the moral sceptic who asks 'Why be good?'. Whereas for the unbeliever goodness seems to be an external circumscription of one's own liberties, an *allotrion agathon*, for the Christian morality is felt as something freely adopted by an internal impulse. Asked why he is good, the Christian answers that he loves his neighbours, and wants to do good by him; asked why he loves his neighbours, he replies that he loves God, and his neighbour is a child of God; and finally asked why he loves God, he explains that he loves God, because God loves him. The sceptical philosopher may niggle, but to the Christian it seems to add up to a perfectly adequate justification of morality. Such justification is not open to the unbeliever, and the Christian finds difficulty in seeing how an unbeliever could rationally choose to observe a moral code. The case put by Glaucon and Adeimantus against morality in Book II of the *Republic* would seem to be unanswerable in purely human terms. The Christian, partly because having known God he does not see how anyone could live without him, partly because having discovered the truth he is inclined to expect and demand rational explanations all along the line, partly, often, because in coming to know God he has become much more conscious of his own self and of natural self-centredness in other men, over-estimates the difficulty other men have in adopting a code of behaviour which limits their self-indulgence and for which they have no adequate *rationale*. But where logic affords no grounds for morality, psychology may yet supply motives sufficient to the purpose. The super-ego may suppress the ego, or a man may make a cold calculation that honesty is the best policy, or his natural inclinations may be weak and lifeless and he may be content to follow the line of least resistance; or he may be muddle-headed enough to think that his moral conduct either has no need of, or has an adequate, justification. In these and other ways men do manage to lead good lives without having any belief in God. The Christian may feel that without faith he could never have lived any sort of good life; but wrongly extends this to think that others likewise cannot be good without God. Yet, incomprehensible though it may be to him, the facts are otherwise. There are decent godless people. He may not be able to penetrate into their minds, but the overt behaviour is there, and proves that it is possible for people to be good, in this limited external fashion, without calling on the aid of God.

The good life, in the limited external sense of the word, is not much of a life. The Christian, who can give himself good reasons for fulfilling its requrements, cannot be content with merely doing that. When one has told the truth, paid one's taxes, observed the highway code, and discharged all one's other normal obligations, one is left with a sense of this being a poor and unsatisfying achievement. Only the love of God can really justify the external good life; but the external good life is no substitute for the love of God. The Christian's conception of the good life cannot stop short at the level of overt behaviour; it cannot stop anywhere short of God himself. But whereas it is possible for me unaided to attain a certain standard of external behaviour, it is not possible for me unaided to attain God. For one thing, God is a person, and all personal relationships are two-way affairs: it is as much a matter of God choosing to have me, as of me choosing to have him. For another, in contra-distinction to human beings, God is an infinite being, and therefore my own, finite resources are inadequate for me to do even my part of the two-way relationship. The metaphor of personal relationships may mislead, because we naturally think of these as between two persons on an equality with each other, but with God, although it still *is* a two-way affair, it is also heavily one-sided. There are two parties, but the human party is not up to much, and it is God who makes most of the going. The human being has it in his power to mar the relationship, but for the rest it is God who makes the relationship possible: he takes the initiative, he unbends, he makes allowances for our limitations, he comes down to our level, or raises us up to his. And therefore, since the Christian regards the good life as being constituted by having the right relationship with God, and regards sin as separation from God, it becomes true, in this extended sense of the terms, that no one can lead the good life without God's special favour, and that without grace all our doings are comprised under sin.

This last facet of the doctrine of original sin does not reflect anything reprehensible about mankind, though perhaps something we may regret. It is not some universal corruption of humanity, but merely a necessary part of the human condition. It is a consequence of autonomy. God made us independent agents, free to choose as we would: we are therefore conscious of ourselves as independent entities, as being ourselves and not anything else. There is therefore a necessary distinction between the agent and everything else, which inevitably gives rise to a sense of separation, and even of alienation. By the mere fact of being created a free and conscious being, I am made aware of my predicament, 'I, a stranger and afraid In a world I never made'. It is not that I have done anything wrong, but simply that, being what I am, I cannot be content to continue being what I am. Being a person in a world of created things, I cannot be happy at merely coming to terms with things; I must fulfil myself as a person with other persons, and above all with that Person who was the Maker of me and of my world. I could not be myself, without being conscious of myself as set apart from everything else: and therefore there is a logical loneliness that I must endure as a condition of being me. I would not avoid this by abnegating my selfhood. I cannot, and would not really want to, if I could, sink back into a state of unreflective sentience, in which I merely responded to simple stimuli, and never had to choose between right or wrong, and was never conscious of myself as an autonomous agent: but I will not convert this logical loneliness into anything worse by adding to the necessary fact that I am a self, the additional one that I am a selfish self, and I would like it if I could come to terms with the rest of reality so that the logical distinction between it and myself was only a logical one and would no more give rise to a sense of loneliness than the fact that they are two persons gives rise to a sense of loneliness in two lovers.

The myth of the Fall represents in symbolic form certain fundamental facts of the human condition. It portrays man as rational (a little) and egocentric (a lot): it tells of our moral and spiritual growing pains in coming to autonomy; and it gives a hint of the restlessness and the spiritual nostalgia that is the consequence of our maturation. Contrary to the Genesis account, the Fall should not be seen as the result of one original sin on Adam's part. No primal decision made us fallen; fallen is what we naturally are. It is a necessary condition of being a man: necessary but insufficient. We could not be autonomous agents at all without having many of the characteristics that have been taken as showing our fallen nature: but our condition is essentially incomplete; being what we are we cannot feel sufficient unto ourselves, but have a lasting urge to make good. The Christian understands our inadequacy and what it is that we lack. He knows that the only really good life is the life lived in the love of God. And he knows further that this is possible. The doctrine of the Fall has been answered by that of the Redemption.

7 ATONEMENT AND REDEMPTION

If the account just given of sin is correct, we need also to rethink our understanding of the redemption. Traditional formulations have been articulated against a doctrine of original sin which stressed the wickedness rather than the nakedness of Adam, and have required of the Second Adam some power of extricating us from the penalties that our ancestor's disobedience had inevitably incurred. We find it difficult to make sense of any such doctrine, partly because our view of punishment is different, partly because we see no natural connection between what Christ did and the remission of penal consequences for the descendants of Adam. Punishment, on our rather non-retributive view, is not essentially attached to wrong-doing, but extrinsically annexed by the edict of a lawgiver or judge, who is perfectly able to remit, for good reason, any penalties that have been incurred, without the need to substitute for them other ills to be borne by a vicarious victim. If Adam, or mankind generally, has aroused God's wrath, then either God is right to continue his displeasure with us, in which case Our Lord's intercession would be an impertinence, or the time has come for him to turn again his countenance towards us, in which case no external action, on the part of Jesus or anybody else, is needed. Certainly, Christ's allowing himself to be betrayed, condemned, and crucified seems quite irrelevant to the legal position of Adam's descendants in the heavenly Courts of Justice.

But the crucifixion does make sense to us. We find it difficult to say what it does mean; but we are moved by it, and feel not only that it was the necessary climax of Christ's life and ministry on earth, but that because of it we are somehow all right with God. If Jesus had not died and risen again, he would still have been a great prophet, teaching us the Fatherhood of God and the Brotherhood of Man; we might still feel called to follow him, thinking, as the disciples did before they knew of his crucifixion, 'To whom shall we go? thou hast the words of eternal life' (John 6. 68). But the Spirit has spoken by many other prophets, and though we Christians find the word of Christ more compelling than those of Socrates or the Buddha, others have disagreed, and we cannot show to their satisfaction that our preference is not just the result of our upbringing. The fact that Jesus died and rose again has always been instanced by the Church as a decisive proof that he was not just a prophet, but more than a prophet, mediating to us the authentic word of God.

Again, without the resurrection, we should have no assurance that the love of God was stronger than the grave. However much we might be inclined to follow the Christian way, we should regard it as being only transiently the life for us, only until we went down to our long home, and were no more seen. It is fashionable to decry immortality. But if there is no resurrection of the dead, and nothing for the individual to hope for, then the Christian message can no longer claim to be one of hope, but only an improved version of Epicurean resignation. If Christianity is to vindicate its claim that God has overcome death then some resurrection was necessary—not perhaps Christ's, but Lazarus' at least.

These two arguments are not direct arguments for the crucifixion, but only for the crucifixion as a prelude to the resurrection. And they do not absolutely require that it should have been the Son of God who should undergo these things. We could envisage a gospel, adequately attested by the miraculous powers of Jesus, in which he showed not only that he was no mere man, but that God could indeed bring people back to life. And yet although this would be good news indeed, it would not be the Good News that Peter proclaimed at Pentecost. It would still be the Old Covenant, in which a distant God told us through the mouth of an accredited spokesman, Moses or Elijah or Joshua-bar-Miriam, what we had to do. And although we might do it, out of deference or awe or prudence or fear, it would be an external obedience to a command from far off, with no sense of liberation or freedom or spontaneity or joy. We should have no sense that in being Christians we were each doing his own thing, each fulfilling his own nature. We could hearken unto Christ, as Jews had sometimes listened to the prophets, but we should not feel all that inclined to follow him, and if we did we should not identify with him, any more than we do with Elijah. Although it *is* good to know that things are not as black as they seem, and that God is in his heaven, and that if we will walk in his ways and follow his commandments, it will be well with us, it is not *that* good. In the light of that news I may see the world as a second Eden, but in the course of time I may be tempted to be another Adam. Even though many of the unpleasing features of this present world—pain, disease, drudgery, and death—could be discounted if we knew that they were but for a reason and that in due course God would wipe away every tear from the eyes of the faithful, we still could become dissatisfied and bored—almost suffocated—in a world in which everything was so completely sewn up, and our actions mapped so exactly. We should feel all the time that we must watch our step; not only, as in this actual world, must we be careful what we do, and make sure not to do anything that would have unpleasant consequences for us, but we should have to exercise equal caution about our inmost thoughts and dreams, since God knows the secrets of our hearts and is as concerned that our hearts should be pure as that our actions should be just. We should not feel ourselves to be cast for the role of children of God, made in his own image, but mere artifacts, at best pets, at worst potter's vessels.

Death is a great leveller; and the fact that Jesus died makes it possible to regard him as one of us, and not simply as a being from on high, who was on an equality with God and came to tell us what God wanted us to do. Christ's mortality is proof of his humanity. Death, like pain, is a great prover of reality. Not only can we allay Docetist doubts that Jesus was only a divine apparition in human form, but we can, more modernly, feel that Jesus was for real, a man of like passions and subject to the same sentence as ourselves, a man with whom we *can* identify. We can identify with Jesus and be one with him, in a way we cannot identify with an idea or a system or an absolute or the ultimate reality, just because he is a man and they are not. And since we can identify with Jesus, we can make his teaching and example our own, and fulfil ourselves in being like him, without any sense of its being an external ordinance he imposed from outside. We can be *en Christo*, whereas we could not otherwise be *en Theo*. We can be incorporated into Christ, and find in his spirit the fulfilment of our own, just because he, being on a level with us, can be one with us, and we can be one with him. Only because he knew the human condition from inside, can we open our hearts to him and share with him our hopes and fears, our aspirations, successes, failures, and frustrations.

Jesus not only died, but died, when and how he did, because of his beliefs. So at least he really did believe them. Many philosophers and men of religion profess very improving sentiments—if one reads Psalm 119 and the Book of Proverbs regularly, it is quite easy to get the hang of it, and churn out suitable sayings for every occasion. But we are all, to a greater or lesser extent, hypocrites, and what we preach is seldom an absolutely reliable guarantee of what we practise or what we really believe. But if a man will go to the stake for something, then, whether we agree with it or not, we have no doubts about his sincerity. And Jesus went to the stake. He may have been mistaken, but whether muddled or mistaken, at least he was sincere. And sincerity is what is most in issue if we are to cast in our lot with someone and identify with him. Many of my friends are muddle-headed and most are mistaken, and none the worse friends for that; but once a man seems insincere the whole basis of friendship is subverted. One cannot trust an insincere man, and trust is essential for fusion of purpose. Even if one believed that Christ was in error in his teaching, it would still be possible to belong to the Jesus people; but not if one believed that he did not believe what he was saying. And the Cross is the conclusive proof that that was not the case.

Adam was alone and lonely. So God gave him Eve. But that was not an adequate cure for the isolation and solitude that autonomy brings. Having eaten of the fruit, they both were ashamed and naked, and both went into exile, having thereafter no abiding city here. And so it is with us. Each man as he discovers himself as an autonomous agent, experiences the logical loneliness of the first person singular; but assuages that loneliness in forming personal relationships with other people and engaging in joint activities with them. The first person singular gives way to the first person plural, and we lose our sense of isolation in doing things together. The moral law loses its exclusive importance for the rational agent, yielding pride of place to personal relationships. It remains important—each of us is continually having to face the question 'What shall I do', and unless he decides it aright the whole of his personal life will go awry—but it ceases to be all-important. Thoughts turn away from oneself to one's family and friends; it is not enough to do what one is told to do or to deserve well of others or of God; one wants to be able to trust them and to feel trusted, to be accepted, to be at one with them, open with them and open to them. The life of morality is filled out by the more satisfying life of personal relationships, and in the company of friends we escape from the solitariness of the individual ego. And yet: all this, though good, is not enough. Our friendships are fragile in the face of reality. We cannot for ever be absorbed in each other—not for nothing did Dante place Francesca and Paolo in hell. As we come to know each other more fully and to achieve a greater identity of experience, understanding, and aspiration, so more insistent becomes the question what we together shall do and how we stand with respect to everything else. As we become more at one with each other, so the first person dual becomes more singular in import, and the two of us together are back in Adam's position. And similarly if we move from the dual to the plural. From Plato to modern socialists, thinkers have sought to alleviate the loneliness, amorality, and *accidie* of the individual by urging him to merge his individuality in some collective greater than himself. The proposal has great emotional appeal. But when we think it through, or if ever it has been put into practice, we find that it cannot take the strain of solving man's moral problems, and that the collective society, as much as the individual, needs some *raison d'être* to inspire it and make its activities seem worthwhile and alive. Plato envisaged a society dedicated to the contemplation of the Forms, and Marxists believe that their society is somehow furthering the dialectical process. Unless we can believe this—unless we can believe that our society is somehow at one with reality and is fulfilling some role in the cosmic scheme of things—collective endeavour is as futile as is that of individuals. And just as individuals in coming to an awareness of their own autonomy experience also a sense of alienation from the universe, so societies suffer sophisticated growing pains as they leave behind the age of innocence and illusions, and know that they, in the same way as individuals, can choose what values to affirm and must bear the ultimate responsibility for that choice. If I as an individual am free, then we collectively are free too; and if I in consequnce suffer from a sense of alienation, so we as a society shall suffer in the fullness of time from a sense of disconnection from reality. And for this reason, personal relations, although an advance on the level of bare morality, and a partial answer to the inevitable isolation of the individual ego, do not constitute a complete resolution of Adam's predicament. If he could feel himself an alien, he and Eve could know themselves to be exiles too; and if I cannot be content to be myself, I cannot get over it by identifying myself with another, not even if that other be of like passions with myself and completely sincere. If Jesus had been merely a man, the Jesus people would have been subject to the some logical inadequacy and would over the centuries have suffered the same attrition as other societies have. However *simpatico* the leader, however satisfying the personal relations that members of the group could enjoy with one another or with him, there still would have been the fundamental fact of freedom to be faced, which when faced would make us all feel very small, shrivelled up and naked before the icy blasts of reality. We might seek refuge in the Old Covenant, as Ancient Israel did. So long as we believed that we had a special role to play, that we were God's own people with a manifest destiny to fulfil, we might for a season be content. But if our content be based on simple obedience to a divine command—if our starting point is simply that God has told us 'If ye hearken to my word and obey my commandments, ye shall be my people and I will be your God', or, more modernly, if we believe that we have been cast for a special role by history, then we must be collectively subject to a heteronomy, or as we might in this case term it, a deuteronomy of the will. The moral law is too external. It is imposed from outside, and although we may, like the Pharisees, be scrupulous in our observance of it, we shall be only whited sepulchres, and inwardly full of corruption. This sickness of soul afflicts not only individuals, but societies as well. In Our Lord's time on earth Judaism was suffering collectively as well as individually. A new prophet might have been able to revitalize it and give it a new lease of life, but only a limited one. Another Elijah could have updated the Law, cut through the legalistic accretions of the Scribes and Pharisees, and reinvigorated men's enthusiasm for it. But as far as prophets were concerned, the law of diminishing returns was beginning to operate. If Jesus had only been another John the Baptist, the New Israel might have been better than the Old, but would not have been essentially different.

The difference between Jesus and John was not that Jesus was done to death—John also was executed—but that Jesus was divine. His death is therefore not only a proof of his humanity and his sincerity, but of God's love. In one way of speaking, we say that God gave his only Son to die for us; in another way, that it was God himself who hung and suffered there. In either case, the crucifixion shows us both what love really is like, and that we are loved by God, not in consequence of any bargain but for ourselves alone. I am no longer to regard myself as a potter's vessel, who, provided I fit into the place God has in mind for me, will be used by God and appreciated by him; nor am I a pet, an additional attraction to the Zoological Gardens of Eden, allowed to exist so long as I behave myself but liable to be put down if I am a nuisance. I am not only made in the image of God, but have value in his eyes independently of anything I do, not depending on his whim or caprice. He cares, to the extent of making the greatest sacrifice he possibly could. And if he cares for us, then it is reasonable that we should care for him. We love him because he first loved us.

The logic of love needs elucidation. We have to show why love provides a non-heteronomous reason for autonomous action which is nevertheless not egocentric or alienated; and why being loved by others is a valid reason for loving them in return. If I love someone I care for him. I want his good, not merely as much as I want my own, but as being my own. This is how love differs from altruism or disinterestedness. A man who pushes the interests of his relatives too zealously is not praised for his altruistic concern for the good of others, but rather criticized for nepotism, which we regard as a form of selfishness. Men identify themselves with their families, and in pursuing their families' interests are pursuing what they see as their own. In the same way men sometimes also identify with their friends, their party, their country, or their denomination, and we recognize the equivocal status of party loyalty, patriotism, or some varieties of the urge to proselytize. This is not to say, as the cynics hold, that these are all vices. Often they are very estimable. But they are not simply forms of unselfishness, even though they are directed towards persons or interests other than oneself. Aristotle's definition of a friend as a *heteros autos*, another self, catches exactly the ambiguity.[1] In personal relationships, concern does not abolish the distinction between different persons, but transcends it. I remain different from you, but we are of one mind in wanting and hoping for those things that are good for you, and in fearing whatever is bad.

---

[1] *Nicomachean Ethics*, IX: 9:10, 1170b6

So they lov'd, as love in twain
Had the essence but in one;
Two distincts, division none:
Number there in love was slain.

Hearts remote, yet not asunder;
Distance, and no space was seen,
'Twixt the turtle and his queen;
But in them it was a wonder.

So between them love did shine,
That the turtle saw his right
Flaming in the phoenix' sight:
Either was the other's mine.

Property was thus appall'd,
That the self was not the same;
Single nature's double name
Neither two nor one was call'd.[1]

Moreover, I want your good intrinsically, not because it is a means to, or concomitant of, my obtaining my own ends. Personal relationships are different from business ones. If I do business with you, I am not trying to do you down, as the cynics suppose, but my good will towards you is conditional and limited. I will keep my side of the bargain provided you keep yours. Your value in my eyes is contingent on your doing certain things, whereby you are of use to me; and the good I am prepared to do you is proportional to your value to me. In the terminology of the Theory of Games, we form a coalition, because we each see that together we can achieve some of our respective interests better than we could separately. But our assessments of the outcome remain separate. Your good is not *eo ipso* my good, and your value in my eyes is simply as a person who can bring good things to me, as a furtherer of my own cause. Anybody else who could do the same would do equally well. I have no commitment to you as you, but only to you as a useful business partner. By contrast, if I have a personal relationship with you, I am committed to you in your own right; you have a value in my eyes because you are you, not because—and only on condition that—you deliver the goods I happen to want. This is what it is to be accepted. You are

---

[1] Shakespeare, *The Phoenix and the Turtle.*

accepted, welcomed, *agapomenos*, when you are valued for your own sake, because you are you, and not simply as someone who happens to be useful. And if you are accepted because you are you, not only is your value in my eyes not conditional and not necessarily limited, but it is also unique. I can do business with anybody, but if I have a personal relationship with you, and value you because you are you, I cannot have *that* relationship with anybody else, just simply because anybody else is not you. To be loved, to be accepted, to be cared for, not only conduces to one's good, but helps constitute one's sense of identity. Although an autonomous agent is necessarily aware of himself as some one separate from everything else, he will be more conscious of his isolation than of his uniqueness, of his solitude than of his significance. Only if he knows that somebody else cares for him, will he be sure that it matters what he does; only if he is accepted, will he have a full sense of his own existence.

Aristotle's definition shows how love transcends the distinction between heteronomy and autonomy. Actions whose original *raison de faire* lay in the will of another are made one's own by love. A young man gathering garlands for his girl and a mother knitting bootees for her baby are both acting entirely spontaneously, voluntarily and autonomously, although young men left to themselves seem to be somewhat insensitive to flowers, and young women do not knit bootees for themselves. In each case the reason for the action is *hetero*, but the acceptance of it as a binding upon oneself is self-imposed and so *auto*. In so far as I accept somebody else, I cease to regard him as altogether other, and make his concerns my concerns. I no longer feel his existence as an alien intrusion on my freedom of action, but welcome it as widening my horizons and enlarging my scope of activity. If he were suddenly to go out of existence, I would not feel more free on account of no longer needing to conform my actions to his needs, wants, fancies, and ideas, but less free, because there would be no longer the possibility of doing things for him or with him. The death of a friend is seen not as a liberation but a loss, and life without him seems not more free but less full, not open but empty. For most people, action on behalf of others comes quite naturally; but for those who are highly self-aware and conscious of their own autonomy, there is the further consideration that self-concern is a wasting stock. If one thinks the matter through or if one attempts to put it into practice, one realizes the vanity and futility of a life lived solely for the sake of one's own self, and so comes to a recognition of a need, not merely natural but almost logical, of something or someone, other than oneself, worthy of one's devotion and service. We need to realize ourselves as autonomous agents, and that requires our discovering both that we are able to do as we want and that we are not content to want only what we happen to want. We are self-directed, but not self-sufficient. In traditional theological terms, we suffer from a conviction of sin. More vaguely and more generally, we are aware of our own inadequacies and our need for some thing, or some one, else. And in most cases this is specified in the service of others, which is seen no longer as an external imposition but as the fulfilment of an inner need. The self, while remaining autonomous, is no longer autarkic, and united to others by love ceases to be solely concerned with itself, but accepts others in personal relationships as equally objects of care and concern.

It takes two to make a friendship. It is perfectly possible for Jack to love Jill, without Jill's reciprocating his affection. And in that case, although Jack may make Jill's interests his interests, she need not in any way identify with him. Yet we feel she should. It is difficult to articulate the argument aright. We are often tempted to argue with my Lady Greensleeves that she owes it to love her lover on account of the many presents and services she has received at his hands—

> I bought thee petticoats of the best,
> The cloth so fine as fine might be:
> I gave thee jewels for thy chest;
> And all this cost I spent on thee.
>
> My men were clothed all in green,
> And they did ever wait on thee;
> All this was gallant to be seen:
> And yet thou wouldst not love me.

But this cannot be right. Not only does it make people commensurate with goods and services, and reduce wives to an exceptionally expensive form of attire, but it entirely destroys the whole nature of love, which must be freely given or it is nothing. Even if we avoid the crudities of the wooer's cost-benefit analysis, and argue that the beloved must love him not on account of his gifts or services, but simply on the grounds of his antecedent affection, our arguments are still too crude, and their would-be compellingness crushes and bruises the bloom they seek to secure. In some important sense, there cannot be cogent reasons for love, since if there were it would not be what we want it to be. I want you to love me not because you have got to, but because you want to. And therefore I cannot reckon that any properties of mine—whether the extrinsic ones of being a good giver of petticoats or the intrinsic one of being your true love—will be adequate grounds for your loving me. For then there would be nothing gratuitous about it, and I should believe that the real object of your love was not me but those properties which constituted the grounds for it; and I want to be loved 'for myself alone and not my yellow hair'. And yet the wooer is not altogether wrong. He cannot compel love, but he can hope to win it. If it were otherwise—if love were given always without any reason whatever—not only would it be pointless to try to acquit oneself well in the eyes of the beloved, but love would not seem all that worth having. A love that was utterly blind would be like a win on the pools—very pleasant no doubt, but not such as to transform or establish the personality. We expect our friends to care about what we do, and to mind if we do badly. Although we do not want to be loved just for our properties, in the sense that anybody else who possessed the same properties would be equally acceptable, yet we think that what we are and what we do is, and should be, important. And so, although we shy away from saying that anybody *must* love anyone else, we do not mean to say thereby that love is utterly irrational, or that no reasons can be given why somebody is loved.

The traditional reason for loving is given by St John: 'We love him because he first loved us', but this is not a simple *quid pro quo*. It is true, as a matter of psychological fact, that smiles provoke smiles and friendliness; and the argument from gratitude is not logically absurd. But in the case of personal relationships there is more to it than that. To be esteemed by another secures one's own self-esteem, and gives body to one's own sense of identity. To know that one is loved is to be able to anchor one's own existence in the affections of others. 'Who am I?' 'I am the person that Mother loves' or 'that Jill loves' or 'that God loves'. It means that my actions matter, not only to me but to someone else in the outside world, and that therefore they have a significance which is not solely solipsistic. Hence from the fact that my existence and my actions have an additional importance, I am led to see them not only from my own point of view, but from another's, and then from both of ours jointly. It begins with vanity, but shades into a sharing of view-points, and ends in a sharing of values. I like being liked, and if other people show that they have a good opinion, I soon come to value the good opinion of others, and thence the opinions of others generally; we exchange opinions and occasionally reach a common mind. Opinions lead to actions, and if we join in forming joint opinions, we shall sometimes join in other activities, and come to use the first person plural as naturally as the first person singular. It is easy to join in, if one is welcome and already accepted; but as one joins in, one shifts, or rather expands, one's view-point, and comes not only to find one's identity in the affection of others, but to identify with them in a stronger sense, and take their interests to one's own heart, and find fulfilment in shared views, values, and endeavours. If I am loved, I am not compelled to love in return; if I am welcome, I do not have to go in; if I am invited, I am not obliged to accept the invitation. But we often do, and if we do, we act with reason in so doing.

The doctrine of the redemption answers that of the Fall. Because we are fallen we have a sense of sin, a logical loneliness and empty vanity that is the concomitant of our being autonomous agents, each aware of himself as a being separate from all others, each in an egocentric predicament. We need to be taken out of ourselves by something or someone other than ourselves, worthy of our devotion. Most people find this in personal relations, a few in dedication to a cause; and in the case of personal relations there is a logic which both transcends the distinction between oneself and others, and makes the antecedent love of another a good reason for loving in return. But in so far as we identify with other people, the fallenness of humanity shows itself again in a sense of communal aimlessness and futility. The first person plural is but the first person singular writ large, and is heir to all the ills that must inevitably beset number one. No purely human gathering can overcome this difficulty. If we, either individually or collectively, are not to feel a sense of alienation and disconnectedness, we need to be at one not only with one another but with God. Only if we love God can we identify with him and do his will not merely because it happens to be his will, but as our own, freely chosen and spontaneously welling up from our hearts. But it is difficult to love God. Why should we? The Old Covenant attempted to answer this question, but gave what were essentially the wrong reasons, heteronomous reasons which might compel our obedience but which for that very reason could not win our love. The New Dispensation is different. There is no *if* about it. God doesn't say, 'If you obey my commandments, then . . .', but shows, simply and incontrovertibly, that he loves us. The rest is up to us. We are not obliged to respond at all, and if we do not, nothing nasty, on our own scheme of values, will happen to us. We are not pressured into loving God; there is no trace of heteronomy. But there is a reason. Not a consequential reason, that good consequences can be seen to follow from loving God, but an antecedent reason, which, although not a compelling reason, is a valid one.

If the argument is correct, the only way we can be released from the egocentric predicament which is the lot of all autonomous agents is to be led out by love, and the only reason we can have for loving someone is his antecedently loving us, and the only way we can know this for certain is by his giving up something valuable for our sakes. The crucifixion enables us to be at one with God not because it is a ransom paid to the Devil, but because nothing less could have brought it home to us how much God cared for us. It was on account of our sin, not as a vicarious penalty, but as the only way of getting it through to us, in our benighted insensitive state, that all the teaching about God loving us was not mere eyewash but was really meant. God so loved the world, that he gave his only-begotten Son, because that was the only way of making his love sufficiently manifest for it to penetrate the isolated and self-absorbed egos of autonomous men. Or, to take the other Trinitarian approach, in identifying with Jesus we are not merely identifying with a human being but also with God. Jesus' self-sacrifice not only shows us what love can cost, but assures us that God is love, and poured out himself for our sakes.

It may seem a blemish to have these two approaches, describing Jesus sometimes as the Son of God whom the Father gave for our sakes, sometimes as God himself, who gave himself for our sakes: but both approaches are necessary. If we had only the former, we might begin to question the reality of the sacrifice, if the Father was going to raise his Son from the dead again. It makes sense normally to think of a son as that which is most precious in a father's eyes, but only on the condition that father and son are both subject to the ordinary limitations of mortality. Abraham really did demonstrate his sincerity by being willing to offer up Isaac, because he did not know of the ram waiting in the thicket, But God the Father could, and knew he could, raise Jesus from the dead, and although he might still have wished to spare his Son the agony and pain and isolation of the Cross, the fact that it would come all right in the end does make a difference. If we concentrate on the actions of the divine Christ, we secure the reality of death, unsoftened by foreshadowings of the resurrection, but lose the bitterness of defeat, the words of dereliction, 'Eloi, Eloi, lama, sabachthani'. Adam was alone, cut off from God. And only if Jesus could be alone, cut off from God the Father—Abba—, could he experience to the full the central facet of our fallen condition: and only if he had experienced that, can we regard him really as one of us, and be at one with him, and through him with God.

8 REASONS FOR LOVING
   AND BEING LOVED

Should a person be loved on account of some of his characteristics or should he, rather, be loved for himself alone? Either way we run into difficulties. If we say that it is the characteristics which constitute the reason why someone should be loved, we seem to be denying his unique individuality, and to be saying that anyone with these characteristics is worthy to be loved. We can guy it by formalizing it in Whitehead and Russell's calculus as

$$(x) [F(x) \And G(x) \And H(x). \to L(x)]$$

where F, G, and H are the characteristics cited and L (x) expresses a person's being lovable or loved: 'for any x, if x is F and is G and is H, then x is to be loved'. But this is to denature personality. You are no longer uniquely you, but merely one among many potential bearers of lovable characteristics. And so you protest and say that you want to be loved not because you are F, G, and H, but simply because you are you. But that too is unacceptable. It divorces your youness from all your characteristics, not only the more adventitious and peripheral ones, but from those which we naturally think of as being most expressive, if not constitutive, of personality. If there be some transcendental ego which alone makes me me, then what boots it to make efforts to do the right thing and cure bad habits? I may not be *merely* what I do, but if my being me has nothing to do with what I do, then what I do loses its significance as being a manifestation of who I am. Although we have, rightly, a sense of a person's being more than a bearer of a few desirable qualities, and hope that at least 'God, my dear, can love you for yourself alone and not your yellow hair', nevertheless, we should not construe this as a straight opposition between loving on account of desirable characteristics and loving not on account of desirable characteristics.

The same difficulty occurs in the active voice. If I give reasons why I love, I seem to deny my spontaneity and authenticity. If I love for reasons R, S, and T, I seem to resemble a tax-payer who, falling into the RST category, is obliged to furnish such-and-such a quantity of love. But if I refuse to give reasons, I save my autonomy at the cost of making myself out to be arbitrary and capricious. 'I love those whom I will love, and I hate those whom I will hate', secures the sovereignty of my will all right, but there is little to distinguish it from the whim of a despotic tyrant.

A lot of the difficulty lies in the use of the word 'reason'. Often we construe it as some sort of sufficient condition, either a cause, antecedent in time, which cannot but bring about its inevitable result, or some legal or social requirement which everyone is obliged to observe. Cupboard love is not real love because it is merely caused, and anyone who feeds the brute will elicit similar tail-wagging responses. The reasons urged on me by my solicitor are cogent, and show why I, or anyone else in my position, must do as he recommends. But just because they are so cogent and universal in application, they are impersonal and inappropriate to the making of decisions about personal relations. I can rationally instruct my solicitor to write you a letter adducing reasons why you should pay your debts to me or keep your cattle from straying on my field, but not to give you reasons why you should marry me or be my friend. If I do this, I only betray my lack of understanding of what friendship or love really is. It is not the sort of thing that you can be manipulated into—like cupboard love; or argued into—as with legal or social obligations.

Reasons should be regarded from both the first—and the second—personal point of view. When I am deciding what to do, I may find myself torn by different considerations, and may be able to articulate the arguments on either side, and in the end say why some outweigh the others. Mostly we find it difficult to articulate our reasons at all fully or precisely, and can only give vague and imprecise accounts of our deliberations; but it is very seldom that we can give absolutely no account at all of what we are doing or why. The normal case is that of the agent being able to give a brief and inadequate, but entirely sincere, account of his reasons, which, so far as it goes, expresses why he made the decision he did, but which falls far short of showing that he, or any one else similarly situated, had to decide in that particular way. Often, however, when I am arguing with you, I am concerned to tell you what *you must* do, rather than opine what, if I were you, I would have done. I try and address to you arguments which shall be completely cogent for you or anyone and which will show that nobody could possibly not do what I say should be done. The standard of proof sought is set much higher. In the first-personal case, I do not claim that the arguments I acted on were compelling, but only that I actually acted on them. I do not say that I had no alternative, but only explain why, of the available alternatives, I picked the one I did. In the second-personal case I am often not concerned to help you feel your way to your own decision—which may take days and days—but aim, shortly and succinctly, to convince you that you have, in the relevant sense, no alternative, and must, but must, do what I suggest.

Cogent arguments cannot afford to be sensitive to personal idiosyncrasies. Although in the second person, they are in the second person plural—or, perhaps better, the second person general not the second person singular; in French, *vous* rather than *tu*. They are therefore too coarse-grained to guide us in personal matters. They have to leave a lot out if they are to be applicable to everyone, and if they are to be completely sewn up, the matters they deal with must be limited to the relatively simple issues which concern lawyers rather than novelists. But although I cannot tell you in the second person why you must love me or anyone else, I can wonder in the first person myself whether I should love you and why. Any reasons I adduce will not be subject to the disadvantages concomitant on cogency. They are only a partial articulation of why I should decide, not a knock-down argument why you, or anyone else, must. And hence there is no suggestion that they must apply not only to me but equally to anyone else. Other people will usually accept my arguments as having some force, but may well reckon there are further considerations overriding the ones adduced. My arguments, partly because they are partial, do not have to be completely theirs as well, and therefore can be exclusively, or at least uniquely, mine. And if, after I have articulated them, somebody tries to universalize them, and make me out as maintaining that whenever R, S, and T apply, one must act in a particular way, I shall be quick to point out that my reasons were not a complete statement of the case, and that in many other situations, even though R, S, and T applied, there might well be other circumstances too which would give rise to counter-considerations. My reasons, being only partial, state only a *prima facie* case, and are inherently open-ended, and therefore can be amplified in a number of different ways, perhaps differently by different people. I am not saying that R, S, and T are together a sufficient condition of its being right to act in a particular way, but only that in a particular, largely unspecified, situation, R, S, and T were, for me, decisive. I am not a tax-payer who, falling into the R, S, T category, am obliged, like anyone else, to give my due of personal affection. Other people, similarly situated, might not find R, S, and T decisive, but be swayed by further considerations U, V, or W. My reasons need not be their reasons, and therefore my having reasons need not derogate from the decisions being mine.

A similar distinction can be drawn in the passive voice. 'You only love me', says the begrudging wife, 'because I cook for you and darn your socks'. The sting is in the 'only'. If true, then personality is being denied. What is valued is not the personality of the wife but her cooking and sock-darning abilities, and if it is only for these that she is loved, then anyone else equally good at producing food and darning socks would do equally well. But it need not be 'only'. I could love my wife for her care and skill in looking after me but not for that alone. It might be one good thing among many, among indefinitely many. Not only for her cooking, but also for her kissing; not only for her cooking and her kissing, but for her good temper, her good humour, her good looks. And so it may go on. Asked why I love someone, I may cite some leading reason, and then to ward off the imputation that it is only because of this I love, hastily add that there are other reasons too. Pressed to say what these are, I can always make a beginning, and yet insist that however much I have already said, there is still more to be said. After a bit, I may be at a loss to say what else it is about a person that wins my heart; but even if I cannot say what else it is, I may still be sure that there is something, and that there is more to the person than all the characteristics I have been able to cite. I may express this by saying that I love you not because you are A, B, and C, but because you are you. But it is a false antithesis. Rather than denying that it is because you are A, B, or C, I should be denying that it is *only* because you are A, B, or C that I love you. Not only because you are ABC but because you are a lot of other things too, some of which I may be able to specify, but many of which I cannot now articulate, but only say that they are features that you possess. It is not just because you are A, B, and C that I value you, but rather because you are that in conjunction with an indefinite number of other features that are characteristic

67

of you. Someone else, who possessed desirable characteristics A, B, and C, would not be just the same in my eyes, because of the indefinite number of other respects in which that other person does not resemble you. It is only in conjunction with them that the characteristics A, B, and C were so decisive, and therefore A, B, and C are not, in their absence, sufficient conditions for anybody else being valued by me in just the same way as I value you.

Individuals on this account are to be characterized by a Leibnizian logic rather than a Russellian. We think of each person or monad as possessing an infinite number of features, partially ordered as regards importance and knowability. Some—shall we say the ability to cook?—are easily ascertained and obviously important. Others are more difficult to discover and are naturally instanced only in a fairly full characterization. Others again are likely to be known only to close friends, and only to them seem a significant part of the individal's personality. At every stage any account of what it is that makes a person lovable will be based on only some initial segment of the infinite list of features that characterize him. Often the account is patently inadequate, but even if it is sufficiently full to be reckoned adequate by everyone who hears it, it will still be less than completely conclusive, and will not constitute what the logicians call a sufficient condition. We shall therefore not be tempted to think that it is simply a finite set of characteristics that is the basis of our evaluation. In so far as it is—and all our knowledge is subject to some limitations of finitude—our evaluation is only tentative. And if we seek to say more definitely why it is that we love a person, although we can specify only a finite list of characteristics—an initial segment of the features of a Leibnizian monad—what we claim is that the real basis of our evaluation is more than this, and that it is on account of all the characteristics of the person in question. We cannot say what they all are, but believe that they individuate uniquely: no other person could have all the significant characteristics the same as you do. And so it is natural to say that I love you because you are you.

9 FRUSTRATION AND FORGIVENESS

The Commission on the Christian Doctrine of Marriage was set up after a debate in the Convocation of Canterbury on 'whether there might be occasions for relaxing the present rule of the Convocation whereby a divorced person with a former partner still living may not have on remarrying a marriage service in church', and attention will be concentrated almost exclusively on its answer to this question alone. It is a pity, but it is significant. It is a pity because there is much of great value in the Commission's report.[1] But it is significant, because it shows the difficulty of reconciling the Church's pastoral concern for those whose marriages have come unstuck with its witness to Christian truth. The Commission has clearly been moved by a great sense of compassion in reaching its recommendation (sections 143–8) that if there were a moral consensus in favour of remarriage it would be theologically well founded, and that, provided there were such a moral consensus in the Church, a divorced person, after 'discreet but adequate inquiry by the competent authority', and a public declaration that he or she is penitent, may be remarried in church. There are many glosses and qualifications, but what will come over will be that the Church has abandoned its traditional loyalty to our Lord's teaching, and accommodated its doctrine to the needs of modern man. Actions speak louder than words. So great is the hardness of human hearts that the careful explanations, discreet inquiries and declarations of penitence will be discounted, and the message will be simply that the Church at long last, like Moses, has recognized the facts of human frailty and modified its doctrines of marriage accordingly. The perceptions of the public are crude and unsubtle: and therefore social institutions have to be simple and unambiguous. We can have dissoluble marriage or we can have indissoluble marriage, but we shall not succeed in having both. We might conceivably be right to adopt Moses' teaching—perhaps we might have misunderstood the New Testament, or perhaps we should not be guided by the New

[1] *Marriage, Divorce, and the Church.* SPCK 1971.

Testament in this day and age, or perhaps, as I have heard one Anglican clergyman maintain, our Lord did not know what he was talking about—but we must be clear that this is what we are doing. The choice is stark, because it concerns not only what the Church says in private in the confessional, but what it teaches in public in a babel of voices where only simple and clear-cut doctrines will be understood.

The Commission argues for a 'high' doctrine of marriage, but not so high a one as our Lord—at least in most people's estimation—held or the Western Church has taught. Our Lord's teaching is dealt with in an appendix, and the view of the Western Church is by-passed in a few sentences. It then becomes relatively easy to argue from hard cases that the Church ought not to take too tough a line with those whose marriages have come to grief. But while the positive arguments of the Commission are admirable, many readers will find their negative ones much less convincing, just because they have failed to take the measure of the arguments on the other side. No doubt some indissolubilists have made an excessively crude appeal to Scripture as though it were a book of statute law, and no doubt others have maintained a metaphysical doctrine of the *vinculum* totally divorced from empirical realities, and no doubt these are bad arguments. But they are not the only ones, nor are they the real ones which have led Christians to believe that no Christian can in the face of God make marriage vows a second time while the first are still being broken.

In Appendix I, 'Jesus on Divorce and Remarriage', Bishop Montefiore examines the New Testament evidence, and in particular discusses the 'Matthaean exception' and 'Pauline privilege' in an illuminating way, which makes clear the complexities of Rabbinical thought in the context of which our Lord taught and the early Church attempted to put his teachings into practice. This examination (pp. 79–90) does nothing to weaken the impression that Jesus forbade divorce, but rather heightens it. In the concluding five pages, however, it is argued that his teaching was not *halakah*, a rule governing conduct, but *haggadah*, edifying exaggeration, appealing to the heart by way of imagination; or at least, some scholars think so; and therefore it may be so, and we cannot 'ground the judgement that all divorce and remarriage is forbidden on the fact that Jesus definitely forbade it' (p. 95). It is an unconvincing argument. It is valid only against those who believe that the Christian religion consists in doing just those things which all modern scholars agree that Jesus enjoined on us in a legislative tone of voice; but few Christians are persuaded either of the infallibility of New Testament scholars or that we should treat our Lord's teaching as though it were an Act of Parliament. Jesus was not a legislator. But he did on occasion tell us what to do, and often showed us why we ought to do it. He did express views about marriage, and was thought by himself and by his hearers to be propounding a more stringent rule of conduct than Moses, and by St Paul, though not by some modern scholars, to have quite definitely forbidden divorce and remarriage.

Though not by some modern scholars—the argument of the Commission here seems to be a straightforward equivocation turning on two senses of the word 'may'. We *may* (in some logical sense of 'may') be wrong in thinking that Jesus meant us to regard marriage as indissoluble—it is an opinion that has been held: but from the fact that we may be wrong, it does not in the least follow that we *may not* (in another sense of 'may') argue from our beliefs. Else, scepticism is the only possible position, for there is hardly a sentence in the New Testament whose authenticity or interpretation has not been denied by some learned theologian. The right procedure is not *first* to ask all academics their academic opinion about isolated texts and *then* argue only from those conclusions on which they are all agreed, but rather to consider the whole thrust of the New Testament and to test tentative interpretations and conclusions against the text, and where they seem satisfactory use them to illuminate the text further, and then to do so the same again and elsewhere. Of course, it is possible that we shall be persuaded that our Lord did not mean that divorce and remarriage were wrong, and if we are so persuaded, then it is clear that we should not, in his name, impose a higher standard than he himself demanded. But if we are not persuaded of this, then from the fact that the contrary view is held, and that therefore it is possible (in some logical sense of 'possible') that we are wrong, it does *not* follow that it is not possible (in a different sense of 'possible'—roughly equivalent to 'rational') to ground our judgement on Jesus' teaching.

In chapters two and three, 'Marriage as a Relationship' and 'The Institution of Marriage', the Commission develops a natural theology of marriage with great sensitivity and insight. Marriage is a natural institution, answering to the deep needs of mankind even in an age of easy contraception and female employment. The third of the 1662 'causes' is, quite rightly, taken as most fundamental, and marriage is seen essentially as a personal relationship 'within which each partner can discover himself or herself through the other, and each can offer to the other the opportunity for healing and growth on the basis of progressive mutual completion' (Section 40). From this it follows that marriage should be exclusive and permanent, and that, although some people have a vocation for the single state, most are called to the mutual commitments of marriage, and this, far from being a second best, is a manifestation in our human lives of the creative and self-giving love of God. In some rather guarded sections (Sections 76–9 and 111–3), the Commission eschews the fashionable unisex view of marriage; there *is* a difference between male and female, and therefore it is right that the promises of the man and the woman should be significantly different. It follows also that marriage is an institution in which both Church and State are concerned, and that proposals put forward by some to distinguish Church marriages from civil marriages are theologically unsound. The Christian doctrine of marriage is not a new law laid on Christ's disciples by Christ, but an insight, revealed to us by him, into the nature of man and of marriage generally. All marriage is God-given; and therefore it is right for the Church, as the servant of mankind, to make its services available even to those who are not practising Christians, because marriage still can be a means of grace; and it would be wrong to aver, as some have suggested we should, that civil marriages are *per se* invalid in the eyes of the Church. No disestablishmentarian solution is possible, because marriage is of its very nature of concern to the Church, but not to the Church alone. The State, and society generally, have a say in it, and may say something different from the Church; but it is the same thing they are all talking about, not different things.

Many Christians will feel that the Commission has not taken the measure of the New Testament evidence; others will feel that the teaching of the Western Church has been given equally short shrift. 'The main objection to the Tridentine doctrine of marriage, however, is that it forecloses the question of indissolubility' (Section 72). But this is a *petitio principii*: no one who is not already convinced that marriage may be dissoluble will regard it as an argument at all. The whole attraction of the *vinculum* view is that it expresses, although in an obscure and unsatisfactory way, the insight that a marriage, like a blood-relationship, is of such a sort that although it may break down, it can never be completely expunged. A child may be abandoned by its natural parents and be adopted and brought up by others: the adoptive relationship may blossom and be blessed with every happiness, and may replace, so far as is humanly possible, the natural one; but still the natural one remains, and may acquire suddenly great significance. Even if I was parted from my brother in early childhood and have never seen him since, he is still my brother, and even now stands in more profound relationship to me than a former playmate would. In the Christian view, the marriage bond is even closer than that of blood. Although we cannot choose whom we shall have as parents, brothers, sisters, or children, we can choose, what is more important still, whom we shall be married to. This choice is, or should be, one of the most significant ones open to men and women. It is, for the reasons the Commission spell out, good that it should be so; but if it is to be so, it requires that the relationship created by marriage should have the same indelible character that blood-relationships have. Else, granted the fickleness of human fancy, to marry will sometimes be, and often seem to be, to establish nothing more than the feelings we sometimes have for our old flames. Men and women, knowing the variability of their affections, want to be able to create a bond more permanent than any of those arising out of the facts of human generation. And as these are, in an important sense, indissoluble, so it must be indissoluble too. Marriages may break down, as other family relationships break down, and cease to be the basis on which people live their lives. Nevertheless, just as blood is thicker than water, a marriage once made cannot be unmade, and it would be a sort of blasphemy to mouth the marriage vows a second time in church while one's previous partner was still living.

But marriages break down; and the sayings of Jesus seem intolerably hard in individual cases. Some second unions seem, so far as we can judge, to be successful, and if once a marriage has broken down and has been dissolved by due process of law, it seems unconscionable for the Church to insist that the parties be told that their Christian duty is to remain single. Many of our enterprises fail, but although the fact of failure cannot be expunged, it can be forgiven. And the Church will, in the judgement of the Commission, be most true to the mind of Christ if it restores those penitent of their matrimonial failures to exactly the same position as those who have not yet embarked on marriage at all. Their first marriage may have been a reality once: but if it has died, we should recognize the fact and clear away the corpse. Nor should we have any qualms about people making in church for the second time promises they have already failed or been unable to keep. For the promises only have meaning within the context of a living marriage relationship, and if that has gone, they cannot be fulfilled and are therefore no longer binding. 'Ought' implies 'can', and therefore 'cannot' absolves from all obligation. Just as the law recognizes that contracts entered into in good faith may become impossible to fulfil, and if thus 'frustrated' can be declared to have no further binding force, so the Church should recognize that marriages entered into in good faith are sometimes for deep psychological reasons, perhaps due to inadequacies of upbringing in childhood, impossible of fulfilment; and then they should be declared to be at an end, and the parties should be released from their undertakings, and be free to make their vows afresh.

It is an attractive argument, but a confused one. The confusion is between the very different pleas, of *frustration*, and for *forgiveness*. There are cases where promises, through unforeseen, unavoidable, and external causes, cannot be discharged, and in such cases the obligations lapse, and he who entered into them is entirely free of them, and cannot be said in any sense to have broken his promise or to have anything to apologize for. There may well be—I think there are—occasions when marriages are 'frustrated' and then the Church should formally recognize this: for example, when one of the partners is 'alive' only as a human vegetable with no prospect of recovery. Such cases, together, perhaps, with those of incurable insanity, and those where a legal presumption of death has been established and the survivor had remarried in good faith, are ones so clearly analogous to death that we should be untrue to the mind of Christ if we did not assimilate them. But then, if there is a second marriage, no act of penitence could be called for—a slightly sombre note, as there must be in all second marriages, seeing that the condition of their occurrence is the shipwreck of the first, but no suggestion of any wrong having been done or needing to be forgiven. The plea of frustration, if it can be accepted at all, must be accepted completely. But we need, like the lawyers, to be very circumspect in accepting it. No foreseen eventuality, avoidable failure, or internal cause can be urged in its support, for it is just to take care of these that promises are made. In particular, most pleas of psychological incapacity are barred. There are plenty of internal psychological senses of 'cannot' in which I cannot do what I ought. But Christ never taught us that we should give in to ourselves, nor called us to a soft life. Christ called sinners to repentence, and to those who really turned over a new leaf he promised forgiveness of sins; and it is primarily as an exercise of forgiveness that the Commission recommends that penitent divorcees should be allowed to remarry in church.

Forgiveness is a difficult topic. We are all sinners, and cannot refuse to forgive others as we hope ourselves to be forgiven; we are all sinners and, given the slightest loophole, will presume on a forgiveness from others which we do not deserve and cannot, until we have entirely disowned our action, really accept. What we normally want, when we ask for forgiveness, is to escape from the natural consequences of our misdeeds. But while it is easy in this sense to repent, it has nothing to do with the radical change of outlook (*metanoia*) that Christ spoke of, which involves not only a reorientation for the future, but a facing of the past, and a willingness to bear full responsibility for whatever has been done wrong. The difficulty is, as the Commission notes, that often we are so inextricably bound up with the ill we have already done, that we cannot, without creating further havoc, escape from the snare. So deep is our involvement with sin that it is often difficult to discern what in individual cases is the right thing to do. We do not tell the tobacconist or bookmaker to give up his livelihood because God wills that we should devote our work to socially useful purposes: should we tell the divorcee to stay single because God wills that marriages should be for keeps? We affirm the sanctity of other family ties, but may in a particular pastoral situation advise a daughter to leave her parents, or parents to turn out a ne'er-do-well son; why should we pretend that a woman who had walked out of a loveless marriage should as a matter of Christian duty abandon a stable but subsequent union and several innocent children to go back to her lawful but unloving spouse? To these rhetorical questions we have no answer. What should the Church's counsel have been to a Christian woman in the Sultan's harem? to a prostitute supporting her aged parents in Hong Kong or Rio de Janeiro? But whatever counsellors or confessors say, they should not so say it that the moral demands of the Christian calling are evaded or our Lord's teaching made out to be mere pious aspirations which people cannot be expected actually to follow. There are dangers in casuistry. Our pastoral concern with the individual case may lead us to dilute the teaching of Christ into a comfortable accommodation to the way of the world. Our Lord did not say to the woman taken in adultery 'Go, make an act of penitence, and, after a Preliminary Declaration, regularize your position'.

The tension between the Church's pastoral and prophetic roles can never be fully resolved. It is inherent in the incarnation that the body of Christ should both be in the world involved in the actual situations in which men find themselves, and yet not be conformed to it. We cannot ignore the fact that some marriages break down; we must not compromise the stringency of our Lord's teaching. In large measure we can avoid contaminating the message of the gospel by qualifications of pastoral expediency, because in the modern world the Church, unlike the State, does not have to hold itself in readiness to provide a decision in every case: the Church is not called upon to decide whether a marriage has suffered irretrievable breakdown, and when a Christian, whose marriage has been dissolved by the State, is wondering whether to embark upon or continue some second stable union, it is often the duty of the clergy not to tell him what to do but to help him make the decision himself what God would have him do. The Commission is right to stress this (Sections 139, 141). But the Church cannot entirely abdicate responsibility. Sometimes a definite ruling is sought. And if a church service is asked for, the Church is being called upon to witness that the union is a marriage as God's Word doth allow, and this we cannot do if we are to be faithful to our Lord. The Church has to make many refusals if it is to maintain the integrity of its witness. Not only money-changers and sellers of doves, but advertising agents, turf accountants and attorneys are forbidden to pursue their avocations within the buildings, or under the aegis of the Church. It may be, as some novelists have suggested, that there is something not only beautiful but positively redemptive about sexual intercourse unconstrained by the formalities of marriage.

But the with-it parson who seeks to bring his teenage flock to church for a love-in is rightly reprobated. It is one thing for the Church to be a Servant Church, marrying and burying the people, and allowing all who are so minded to pray and praise and give thanks within its walls; it is quite another for it to be an accessory to sin, and to compromise by its compliance the rigour of God's requirements of men. And if the Church makes itself available for those who have made and broken their marriage vows once to make them in exactly the same words a second time, it will be saying in unmistakable terms that these words do not mean what they say, and that a broken marriage is only a regrettable incident along the road of life.

If we reject the Commission's recommendations, what should we do? I do not know. So far as the argument from witness is concerned, the case would be met by the Orthodox provision for a different penitential rite for second marriages. Certainly the arguments adduced against it (Section 143) are unconvincing. And always the blessed principle of *oikonomia* is at hand to temper the asperities of doctrine to the individual case. But so far as the doctrine of marriage is concerned, I believe the Western rather than the Eastern position is the true one, and that although people whose marriages have broken down may enter into other stable unions, they cannot enter a second time into that state of unqualified lifelong commitment which alone, in Christian eyes, can be called a marriage. The difficulty is partly one of semantics. Divorcees who have been remarried in a Register Office are not notorious evil livers who ought to be excommunicated, and it is not for the Church to say that their unions are not blessed in the eyes of God. But if we are pressed to say that they are marriages in accordance with the will of God, and in particular if we are pressed to allow them to be solemnized as marriages in church, it seems to me that the only answer we can truthfully give is No.

10 FORGIVENESS

What is it to forgive someone? Under what conditions ought we to forgive? Or ourselves to seek forgiveness? Our attitudes are confused. We think we ought to forgive, because Our Lord told us to, but have little idea of what is involved, or how forgiveness is linked with penitence, pardon, punishment, reconciliation, and other related concepts.

Only wrongdoing can be forgiven. It makes no sense to say 'I forgive you', and when you say 'What for?' reply 'Oh nothing; I just thought I would forgive you'; nor would it do to instance some meritorious or morally neutral act as one for which a man is being forgiven. Just as I can only punish you for something you have done which is, at least in my eyes, wrong, so I can only forgive you for what are regarded, at least by me, as your misdeeds.

The comparison with punishment is both illuminating and misleading. If I can punish you, I can also pardon you. It may be that you have done wrong, and deserve to suffer wrong in consequence, and that I am the person authorized to impose some appropriate penalty upon you, and yet I refrain from so doing, and as an act of mercy or on account of some consideration of expediency pardon you and remit the penalty. It is tempting to construe forgiveness as a spiritual analogue of pardon; and so it sometimes is, but not necessarily or essentially. For to see forgiveness as a form of private pardon is to miss its essentially personal and non-legalistic character. If the Lord's Prayer merely advocated a universal leniency it might make the world a better place, but it would not express the heart of Christ's hopes about men's relationship with one another and with God. Forgiveness would become only an easy-going indifferentism, a willingness to let live that we might also be allowed to live as we liked without restriction or hindrance. It might be good policy, but could never be the Good News, only a Laodicean latitudinarianism.

If a person does wrong, we cannot endorse his action. He made up his mind to do it, but we are not of one mind with him in the matter. We cannot identify with him in his acting thus, and it therefore stands between us. If it is some minor action, we may well forget it with the passage of time—and often misdeeds are better forgotten than forgiven—but some actions are too grievous and too fundamental to be quietly brushed under the carpet. They rankle, and the memory of them poisons the atmosphere. A man who could do them, we feel, can be no friend of ours. They are a barrier between us, and it is difficult to see how it could be otherwise, if what was done was important and was meant and is regarded by us as very wrong. And yet; all need not be over between us on account of misdeeds, bad though they may be. We may still want to be one with him, even though we cannot connive at his wrongdoing; and he may come to want to be at one with us, even though he cannot undo what he has done. Just as it is possible to change one's mind before the event and not do what one had decided to do, so it is possible to change one's mind, though not the course of events, afterwards, and be no longer minded to act as one had in fact acted. One can wish one had not done what one had earlier quite deliberately decided to do. And one can do more than merely wish. One can disown one's action entirely, changing one's whole mind about it, rethinking it through and carrying out one's fresh intention to the full: in Greek, *metanoia*.

I can only disown what I already own. Hence the necessity of owning up. I must own up to myself, to other people, to God, for what I have done. I must acknowledge what it is that I did, that it was I who did it, and that it was wrong. Until I have been honest with myself, my change of heart will be merely superficial. It is easy to regret one's decisions when they miscarry—but what is regretted is not the decision, the frame of mind in which the choice was actually made, but the consequences. Only when I fully recognize what I have done can I begin retrospectively to unwill it. I cannot undo it, but if I really now unwill it, I shall try to make good the damage I have done, and attempt to regain the course I ought not to have abandoned. It may not be possible. Many damages can never be made good, and compensation is often woefully inadequate. Many opportunities once missed never recur and often I must live with the consequences of my folly and my evil-doing. Nevertheless, there are invariably some remedies, partial though they are, that can be undertaken, and some new leaves that can be turned over. And in so far as I cannot undo or make good what I have done, I can at least show willing by taking on some extra burden or obligation, as it were making it up some other way. Of course, it is not really making it up. There is no ledger of profit and loss whereby I can set some new-found merits to pay off old debts. But I can make manifest my change of mind by not being content to let bygones be bygones, but making all the more evident and all the more real my concern with other men's good in view of my neglect of it in time past. It is very difficult to disown one's actions. A verbal apology is by some too easily made to cut much ice. Deeds speak louder than words. If it lies within my power, I should make good the damage done by my misdeeds. But often there is nothing I can do to mitigate or compensate for what I have done, and still I want to do something as a more substantial declaration of new intent than mere words can achieve.

Penance is not punishment. The two are alike in being necessarily unpleasant and necessarily imposed in view of past wrongdoing: but punishment is imposed by another, some special representative of an established moral or legal code, as a sanction against breaches of that code by anyone; whereas penance is self-imposed, or at least freely accepted by the wrongdoer as a token of his penitence, his repudiation of his previous actions, or better, of his previous self. Punishment can be inflicted on a man whether or not he admits its justice; penance, unless freely undertaken, is meaningless. Punishment can be concerned with other men besides the actual wrongdoer, and other actions besides the wrong actually done; penance is concerned exclusively with the penitent and solely with his past misdeeds now being disowned. We can admit considerations of deterrence, prevention, and reform to our theory of punishment, but they have no part to play in the concept of penitence, which can only be undertaken by the penitent as a token of his contrition. It is purely symbolic, because if there is anything effective a man can do to repair the damage caused by his wrongdoing, he needs already to have done it before he can be said to have disowned his action at all. It is only when he has done all that he can do to make good, and feels that that is still not enough, that the question of doing something more, in order to make up for what cannot be made good, arises. Penitence is purely symbolic, because anything else is already accounted as restitution. That is not to say that penitence cannot be effective in securing some other good. If I have killed someone by dangerous driving, after I have done everything I can to provide for his widow and children, I may undertake some voluntary work for immigrants in token of the abhorrence with which I regard my former disregard for human life. It is a worthy labour and may be effective in doing good: but *vis-à-vis* my homicide it is purely symbolic. It cannot bring the dead man to life nor compensate his dependents. And not until I have done the latter to the best of my ability should any question of further expressions of penitence on my part arise.

If penance is merely symbolic, it may seem otiose; and often it is. It is an expression of my change of heart, but to whom? To the man wronged? But if I have both expressed myself in words and, by undertaking restitution, in costly deeds, what need is there for further proof of my sincerity? There is a danger that a profuse apology and a small token of regret will be proffered instead of a full and proper reparation. To the public? But what business is it of theirs? Sometimes it is—although my actions may have hurt only a few people, they may have offended many—and in the nature of the case the public need not know of the reparations I have made, so that some symbolic gesture may be in point—say a contribution to a named charity—but, at least in our culture where we dislike losing face, a public apology is in itself token enough of a sincere change of heart. To myself? There is more point in that. I am often at odds with myself, the more so when I have been doing wrong. I may need to show myself, in order to assure myself, that I really do mean what I say. Words, including my own words, go in at one ear and out of the other. Only in action do I ensure that however divided my soul is in its aspirations and motives, when it comes to the crunch it is my better self that has the upper hand. So penance may be in point. But the heart is deceitful above all things, and can easily turn penance to dishonest ends, pretending that by reason of having done a small penance it is really penitent and has shed its previous habits and escaped the evil consequences of past misdeeds. Penance may be the pledge of amendment of life that the divided mind needs to give itself, but can be a further cloak that it uses to conceal its real situation from itself. To God? But the sacrifice of God is a broken and a contrite heart. God knows the secrets of my heart, and needs no actions to convince him that my words are meant.

God does not need persuading. If a man has turned away from

his wickedness, God knows it, and will accept it without any further extrinsic token of contrition; while if he is not really sincere in his penitence no number of penances will deceive God. God's willingness to accept a man's change of heart should not be taken as a matter of course. Regrets—even genuine Greek *metameleia* and *metanoia*—are quite unable to undo the past, and if past wrongdoing by one party has ruptured the relationship between him and another, he may disown the action as a necessary condition of restoring the relationship, but cannot assume that it is a sufficient condition. It takes two to repair a relationship, just as it takes two to make one; and although if a man acknowledges his responsibility and compensates us for the damage he has done to us, we have no further claim against him, we might still feel bruised, and somewhat wary of him for the future; particularly with men, whom we know by bitter experience to be very much creatures of habit, and for all their protestations liable to repeat their failings when further occasions arise. We cannot easily forget, nor should we. That which a man has done once he may do again. We do not go on punishing the peculator—but do not employ him again in a position where he has to handle money. Even if a man seems sincere in his determination to turn over a new leaf, we retain a residual doubt which constitutes a formidable barrier to his being again admitted to complete intimacy. He may have disowned his action completely, but still we hesitate to identify with him again. Beyond a certain point we cannot legally or morally claim further damages; but even when the last farthing has been paid, we are not obliged to readmit a man to our friendship, for the same fundamental reason as precludes our being obliged to admit anyone to be a friend in the first instance, namely that friendship is not a matter of obligation but a favour of free choice.

Most Christian thinking about forgiveness has been either too soft or too hard. The soft doctrine of forgiveness—the one most in fashion in this present age—construes forgiveness as a general indifference to what other people do. If people do wrong and tender their apologies—or even if they do wrong and do not tender their apologies—we should not mind, and carry on regardless. And, of course, there is much pastoral wisdom in teaching people so. Most things that most people do most of the time do not matter very much, and apologies should be offered and accepted as part of the courtesies of life without more ado. Perhaps they are sometimes somewhat insincere—'Please forgive me for my delay in answering your letter'—but no matter. Scrupulosity is more un-Christian than easygoingness, and serious-minded people need to be taught to make light of other people's peccadilloes. Yet not all wrongdoing is unimportant, and we miss the urgency and immediacy of Christ's teaching if we make out that nothing other people do ever matters, and that we should never mind what they have done but always be ready to let bygones be bygones. It does matter what people do. If I do not mind what you do, it shows that I do not care for you—that you are nothing to me; and if I am brought up not to mind what other people do it means that they are all aliens to me and I am isolated among them. I need to identify, if I am to fulfil my nature as a social being. And if I am to identify with you I must evaluate your actions in the same light as I do my own, and therefore find your wrong actions, if they really are seriously wrong, a bar to continued identification. It is good for brethren to dwell together in unity rather than to live separate lives each merely minding his own business; but unity is fragile, and must be vulnerable to serious wrongdoing on the part of any one member of the brotherhood; else it is not a real unity at all but merely a civil façade over an essential separateness of spirit. In enjoining forgiveness, we are not telling people to take no notice of what other people do, although we may urge them for their own sakes not to indulge in rancorous feelings towards those who have done them wrong. We may, that is, urge a man who has been wronged by another not to keep thinking about it, because although it was a grievous wrong, there are many other better things to think about, and he ought not to dwell unnecessarily on unprofitable topics. But we cannot urge him to forgive him so long as he has not disowned his action and sought forgiveness.

Christians of earlier generations often erred in the opposite way by having too tough a doctrine of forgiveness. They were overwhelmed by a sense of man's littleness and God's goodness, and the enormity of man's supposing that he could get away with defying God's will, and could expect still to be admitted to God's good books. Underlying this doctrine is a conflation of a number of different insights: that God's standards are very much higher than man's, so that almost nothing I do can be good enough for him; that man's motives are mixed and his heart corrupt, so that his repentance is seldom truly sincere; and, above all, that forgiveness, like friendship, is a favour not a right. It is easy to express these insights by assimilating the language of penance and forgiveness to that of penalty and pardon; but penalties, if not remitted, can be paid, and once paid cannot be further exacted; whereas, since no amount of penitence and penance can force forgiveness, we are led to view the penalties imposed by God's justice as being disproportionately severe in order to be commensurable with his mercy in pardoning us and restoring us to his favour. What has gone wrong is that we are attempting to express insights about personal relationships in essentially inappropriate legal terms. Forgiveness is not a legal concept, a sort of celestial pardoning, but a personal one. We cannot be forgiven as of right, any more than we can be favoured with God's friendship in the first place as of right. God is not obliged to like us or regard us as his children any more than we are obliged to like one another or regard one another as brothers. But God does, as we, on occasion and to a limited extent, do. What disrupts our relationship with God is our actions and attitudes, sometimes big bad actions or more commonly the whole pattern of our behaviour, just as our actions and attitudes often disrupt our relationships with our fellow men. In both cases our misbehaviour, although fatal, is not final. It can be enough to make everyone want to break with us, and once done cannot be undone. But it can be disowned. And if it is disowned, then not only does it become possible for the relationship to be restored, but, in the case of God (we are told by Jesus) it will be restored, not because he has to or is obliged to, but because he wants to. There is an antecedent desire on God's part to identify and be identified with us, which leads him to seek both to establish and to restore his relationship with us. All that is required for it actually to come about, is that we should desire it too. But if we equally want to be at one with our fellow men, then we will not allow their past but now disowned misdeeds to stand between us, and will be anxious to forgive as soon as we can. And so we can say, 'Forgive us our trespasses as we forgive them that trespass against us'.

11   CHILDLIKE MORALITY

Professor Nowell-Smith claims[1] that religious morality is infantile, that is, that many elements of our morality, especially those peculiarly associated with religion, are hangovers from our childish experience before the age of five, and between the ages of five and nine. I do not want so much to controvert Professor Nowell-Smith's thesis as to complement it. Most of what he says is true, and needs to be far more widely known by Christians than at present. My aim as a Christian is, rather, to make some further points about the Christian understanding of man and morality, so as to show that Professor Nowell-Smith's thesis, instead of being against Christian morality, is essentially consonant with it.

Professor Nowell-Smith criticizes the rule-bound character of many religious codes. Quite rightly. But Christ and St Paul made the same criticism long before. The very slogan that Professor Nowell-Smith chooses to fight under—'the Sabbath was made for man, not man for the Sabbath' (pp. 8/99)—was first uttered by Christ (Mark 2. 27). Christ it was who, holding the same high ideal of monogamy as that put forward by Professor Nowell-Smith (pp. 21/112), nevertheless refused to condemn, as Professor Nowell-Smith would refuse to condemn, the woman taken in adultery (John 8. 11). Christ is much harder than Professor Nowell-Smith on the conventional morality of the conventionally religious; he does not merely deprecate them as infantile or immature, but damns them as dead—whited sepulchres (Matt. 23. 27). St Paul is more concerned with the Law, and has more of a theory about it, than what has come down to us of our Lord's saying; but from the multiplicity of his utterances, one thing at least is clear: he is not a deontologist in Professor Nowell-Smith's sense, 'The letter killeth, the Spirit maketh alive' (2 Cor. 3. 6).

It would be too easy a triumph to point out that Christian morality is not at all what Professor Nowell-Smith says it is, and is as much concerned to controvert what he is trying to controvert

[1] P. H. Nowell-Smith, 'Morality: Religious and Secular', *Rationalist Annual* (1961), pp. reprinted in I. T. Ramsey, ed., *Christian Ethics and Contemporary Philosophy* (London 1966), pp. 95–112.

as he himself is. For it is a sad truth that most professing Christians are in fact practising Pharisees, all Christ's own teaching to the contrary notwithstanding. Moreover, not everything Christ said would meet with Professor Nowell-Smith's approval: 'Except your righteousness exceed the righteousness of the scribes and Pharisees, ye shall in no case enter into the kingdom of heaven' (Matt. 5. 20). Christian morality, as Professor Nowell-Smith concedes (pp. 9/99), is a fusion between Greek and Hebrew types of morality, and the New Testament Christian does not reject the Old Testament in the way a modern humanist thinks he should. I shall try to explain why.

The Old Testament is not simply a set of commandments and laws, though Judaism became largely just this: its primary theme is the growing sense of the inexorability of God, a greater and greater awareness of a reality other than oneself, making for good. The peculiar tone of religious morality stems from this sense of the objectivity of values. Just as my believing something does not make it true, so my choosing something does not make it good: and just as I find myself under a relentless pressure to discover what the truth is, so equally I feel an unremitting urge to seek out and perform whatever it is that I ought to do. Some humanists believe in the objectivity of values too, but they take exception to the uncompromising stringency of the demands which the believer believes God to make on him.

The Christian differs from the humanist not only in believing in God, but in disbelieving in man. The Christian holds that men are always imperfect: that though their aspirations may be infinite, their achievements are always limited. The Kantian ideal of the entirely autonomous man is only an ideal. Being the mere mortal clay that we are, we never do have and never shall have holy wills. The Christian is deeply imbued with a sense of his own fallibility. Although each of us is autonomous in the sense that only he can make up his own mind, it does not follow from a man's having made a decision, that he has made it rightly. And our decisions not only may be wrong, but quite often are. Autonomy for the humanist is a standard of adult behaviour which most men do, or can, attain; the Christian does not believe that men can attain an adequate standard. We may—some men do—grow better with the passage of time; but to the end of our lives we remain something of the child in moral matters; still growing, perhaps, but never grown up; capable often, perhaps, of acting rightly, but always capable of being wrong. For the humanist 'adult' and 'infantile' are polar terms, and 'adult' is clearly a pro-word, and 'infantile' a con-word: the Christian does not regard 'child-like' as a pejorative word. 'Unless ye turn and become as little children, ye shall not enter into the kingdom of heaven' (Matt. 18.3). By comparison with the Kantian ideal of autonomy, we are none of us fully adult; and though we should aspire towards being as adult as may be, we ought always to recognize that we have not reached in moral matters a level of complete adulthood.

The Old Testament element in Christian morality reflects also the fact of man's being imperfect. We need the moral law, St Paul can be roughly rendered (Gal. 3.23), because we are not adult enough to take our own decisions correctly. But when, and if, we come to a full knowledge of God's love, then we shall be emancipated from the shackles of the law, and shall be able to enter the full freedom of the Christian who takes all his decisions for himself, and being filled with the spirit of love takes them all correctly. St Paul sometimes talks of complete emancipation coming at a man's conversion to Christianity; but occasionally speaks as if even converted Christians see through a glass darkly, and only in the next world face to face. I think the latter view is right. It is not in the nature of finite man to know as he is known.

If we only know in part, then our decisions, being based on partial knowledge, are not fully rational. Often the father lets the child go its own way, and learn by its mistakes, but sometimes he lays down a ruling, the reason for which is beyond the comprehension of the child, but which the child is nevertheless required to obey. To me it seems obvious that one's attitude to an omniscient and loving being should be the same. The Christian, just turned twenty-one, is enjoined to follow the Christian teaching on, say to take the most unpopular example, sexual morality in the same spirit of blind obedience as that in which at an earlier stage he followed his mother's injuctions about washing behind the ears. It is not, as Professor Nowell-Smith suggests, the arbitrary edict of a capricious being, but rather the wise instructions of an infinitely far-sighted one. Many men come in the end to believe with Professor Nowell-Smith that monogamy is the best and happiest form of life; and not a few will testify that chastity supports and supplements monogamy. But few adolescents really believe them, nor every adult; even among the middle-aged there are some who are tempted to break up their marriages, and will regret it if they do. The Christian code is clear and firm on this point. Of course it is not enough, as Professor Nowell-Smith points out, to secure the happiness of a marriage; nor would it be necessary to lay it down at all if we were all the time fully apprised of the pattern of life we wished to live and the means required to secure its realization. But for men, such as we actually are, often inconsiderate, often lustful, often impatient, the seventh commandment is a helpful instruction.

The basic objection Professor Nowell-Smith has to Old Testament morality is the element of blind obedience in it. The Christian is prepared to do things for no other reason than that God tells him to do them, whereas the humanist believes that the only acceptable moral actions are those whose *rationale* is transparent, those which can be seen to befit a pattern of life accepted as a goal (pp. 21/111). This objection can be largely met by a consideration of a disposition Professor Nowell-Smith does approve of, loyalty (pp. 20/110). For, though I cannot set out a precise list of acts that constitute loyalty or disloyalty, it seems to me to be the essence of loyalty that one trusts the person one is loyal to *beyond* the limits of one's own knowledge. I show my loyalty to someone when I do a thing which he wants me to do and which I would not have done on my own account, when I believe in him and accept his judgement without being able to justify it in the particular case under consideration. To believe one's friend when one can see for oneself that what he says is true is not to show any loyalty towards him; one would do that much for anyone, friend or foe alike. Loyalty, like faith, is an essentially heteronomous idea. It involves being ready to say, 'Not as I will, but as thou wilt' (Matt. 26. 39) (pp. 13–14/104). Churchill showed his faith in, and loyalty to, Roosevelt when in 1940 he made a sacrificial sale of Courtaulds' American assets to the United States Government (*Second World War*, Vol. II *Their Finest Hour*, p. 506). It was certainly not something he would have done if he had been acting according to his own judgement nor something for which he could see any justification at the time of the request. This I would offer as a paradigm case of loyalty in place of that of Abraham and Isaac. The story of Abraham and Isaac confuses the issue because it was originally told to a people who had not yet realized that human sacrifice was wrong, who had not yet been told that they should not offer the fruit of their body for the sin of their soul. It is the sacrifice of Abraham's affections, not of his scruples, that the story is meant to illustrate. How far one should be prepared to sacrifice one's scruples out of loyalty is a difficult question—if an inquisitor had done violence to his conscience, and had allowed a heretic to escape the flames out of deference to divine commands, I am not sure that we should be categorical in our disapproval—but this is a question I do not want to discuss. I only want to make two points: first that some degree of loyalty, faith, obedience, trust, is a necessary virtue for non-omniscient, finite, fallible beings, such as we ourselves are, if we are to have any relations with other beings, and are not to be utterly autarkic and sufficient in ourselves. And secondly, that the obedience demanded of a Christian, although blind in the particular instance, is not without a general justification. The Christian is told to be chaste, to be long-suffering, not to impute bad motives to other people, irrespective of whether he can see how these characteristics fit into a desirable pattern of life, or may be justified in any other way. But his obedience and loyalty to God are themselves justified by his belief that God loves him. Much has to be taken on trust, so much that some people's faith in God is severely strained. But the obedience demanded of the Christian is not utterly blind. Faith is not (*pace* many Protestant theologians) arbitrary. Although we are told not to expect God to justify his ways to us to our own satisfaction, we have a fair token of his general good will towards us in his willingness to undergo the agonies of death upon the cross. The non-Christian will reject that this actually happened, but that does not affect the *logic* of the Christian's position. The Christian's loyalty, although complete and unswerving, is not groundless or arbitrary. He has his reasons for believing in God and in his goodness towards us, though he is not in a position to constitute himself a supreme court to adjudicate the moral worth of God's every edict and action.

The great merit of rules and commands is that they are fairly precise. I know how to keep the rules and obey commands long before I am able to carry out the agapaistic policy of loving God and doing what I like, and whereas there may be many disputes about what the best pattern of life is, or wherein the greatest good of the community lies, there is little room for dispute on whether one has committed adultery or whether one has broken the speed limit. And therefore we make use of rules, in spite of all their many disadvantages noted by Professor Nowell-Smith, both for propaedeutic purposes and in promulgating legal and social codes. In so far as the Christian Church is a corporate body with social organization of its own, it has rules and regulations, just as any other community does; and because Christians regard their moral and spiritual education as never complete, they never claim that Christian teaching can be dispensed with. There are dangers in making use of rules. What was intended to be a signpost can become a straitjacket, and men are all too ready to regard the observance of rules as a sufficient condition, instead of merely a necessary condition of trying to live according to a certain ideal in common with other men. Many churchmen have been deplorably rule-bound. What gives Professor Nowell-Smith's paper its point is that what he is attacking corresponds so often with the actual practice of Christians: but not the practice of Christ nor the teaching of the Christian Church. And though Christ and the saints go much further than Professor Nowell-Smith would approve in accepting the necessity of rules and in regarding obedience as a virtue, it is far from clear that in this he is right and they are wrong.

It is difficult to pinpoint the Christian's disagreement with Professor Nowell-Smith. So much of what he says can be found in Christ's sayings and St Paul's writings, that it is tempting to claim him for an unwitting believer instead of a convinced adversary of the Christian faith. Yet to do this would be to do scant service to the truth, and I want to end by attempting to summarize the heads of agreement and disagreement between Christians and humanists. There is substantial agreement on the content of morality, 'that love, sympathy, loyalty and consideration are virtues. . .' (pp. 5/95), though Christians lay greater stress on loyalty and humility than would Professor Nowell-Smith. Christian teaching is as insistent upon the dangers of mere rule-observance as Professor Nowell-Smith could want, though many Christians are heedless of the warning, and are as infantile in their religious outlook as Professor Nowell-Smith maintains. Christians are, however, a good deal readier to recognize the necessity of having rules than Professor Nowell-Smith would be himself. This is because Christians take a very much lower view of themselves than do humanists. They do not think that because they choose to do something, therefore it is right. On the contrary, the Christian believes that most of his unaided choices would have been likely to land him in chaos. The Christian differs from the humanist, therefore, in having a much livelier sense of the difficulty of leading the good life or of coming to the knowledge of the truth. He differs also from some humanists at least, and from all sceptics, in having an overpowering conviction that, incompetent though he is, there is a truth to be discovered and a good life to be lived; and these for him are based on his belief in God, and therefore are an absolute 'must'.

12 CHRISTIAN MORALITY

Of the questions that vex moral philosophers, the two most substantial are: How do I know what I ought to do? and, Why ought I to do it?, and to these two questions Christianity has its own answers. To deal with the latter first, the fundamental reason why I ought to do what I ought to do, is because I love God, and doing what I ought to do is an expression of my love of God. And the reason why I do, and should, love God is that God loves me, and gave himself, in the form of his Son, Jesus Christ, to die for me and for all mankind. We love him, because he first loved us.

Many philosophers will object to this fundamental justification of morality. Some will say that it is otiose—they will point out that it is a tautolgy that one ought to do what one ought to do, so that there is no real question; others will say that it is impossible—individual moral judgements can perhaps be justified, but morality in general can no more be justified than, say, deduction; others, again, will object to the form of justification, which adduces some sort of fact, that God loves us, in support of an evaluative conclusion, that we ought to act in certain ways.

To deal with the last objection first, that the love of God, being some sort of fact, cannot lead us to accept any moral principle, is ill founded. It rests upon a confusion between deduction, properly so called, and derivation in some wider sense. It is true, as Hume says, that 'ought's cannot be deduced from anything other than 'oughts': but this is something about deduction generally, which is essentially tautologous and can never contain in the conclusion anything which was not already in the premisses. We cannot deduce evaluative conclusions from factual premisses: but then neither can we deduce factual conclusions from analytic premisses: nor general conclusions from particular premisses. The truth is that deduction is a very limited mode of reasoning. It has enjoyed undue attention from philosophers because it was discovered first and is easy to formalize; but, outside mathematics, it is not a mode of reasoning we commonly employ. Most of our arguments are non-deductive, but are none the worse for that. In particular our moral arguments are non-deductive; in arguing about moral matters we commonly do adduce matters of fact and on them base our contentions in favour of particular moral conclusions. In this way we do derive 'ought's from 'is's. Therefore if it is claimed, as it often is by Hume's followers, that one cannot derive an 'ought' from an 'is', we must ask what is meant by 'derive'. If 'derive' means 'deduce', then the claim is true, but trivial; if 'derive' means something like 'justify' or 'argue from', then the claim is false. We do derive 'ought's from 'is's constantly. And to say that we cannot is simply to take up, in concealed form, a position of moral scepticism.

The first two objections also represent strongly held views, which no doubt accord with the intellectual experience of many thinkers, who may well have found it unnecessary or impossible to justify morality. Nevertheless it remains also a fact that moral scepticism is quite a common experience. Many people, particularly as they grow up, find that though they can operate their moral concepts quite competently, and are in no doubt about what they 'ought' in some sense to do, this 'ought' fails to get a grip on them, and they do not see any really good reason for doing what they 'ought' to do. Such scepticism is a general scepticism. It is not met by redeploying the arguments in favour of particular moral doctrines. The arguments are already known, their strength already acknowledged. As arguments go, they are allowed to be good ones, but none of the arguments thus far produced is felt to be good enough actually to bear on the agent's will. The agent, conscious of his own autonomy, feels himself detached from all arguments and reasonings. He can observe them but is not involved in them or swayed by them. The failure, if it is a failure, lies within the agent, who finds himself unable to be convinced, rather than in the particular arguments for particular doctrines which are as convincing as moral arguments can be; so the remedy, if there is one, must be such as to win again the agent's allegiance to the web of obligations he has been able to see but unwilling to accept. The love of God is such a cure. It can overcome the isolation of the self-willed self, and lead him back into companionship with his fellow beings. Love naturally elicits this response. It is a common fact of experience how the love of a woman for a man can bring him out of himself and bring out in him a humanity and sensitivity to others that had hitherto lain hidden. The love of God is like human love in this, only it is more lasting in time and infinitely patient. It can go deeper than can human love, and not only can cure the temporary sense of separateness and solitariness, which many men often feel, but can overcome the metaphysical loneliness that an autonomous rational agent must know, by affording him the one good reason he must acknowledge why he should commit himself unreservedly, to something, or rather somebody, other than himself.

It is thus both necessary and possible to justify morality in the face of moral scepticism. The love of God is such a justification, and I believe in the long run the only entirely adequate one. There are other justifications—the hope of heaven and the fear of hell among religious ones, a calculation that honesty is the best policy, and the fear that dissolute behaviour leads to psychological ill-health among worldly ones, an acceptance of some doctrine of the categorical imperative or of the higher self among philosophical ones, to mention only a few. Moreover, very many people will accept a code of morality without justification—it is this that has led philosophers to suppose that no justification was called for or could be given. Precept and example are enough to get most people to adopt a code of right conduct. Although man has always been worried about the moral education of his sons, and how to bring them up to do the things he thinks are right, and although people have always felt that the younger generation was going headlong down the path to ruin, moral standards have been handed on with remarkable success. Traditional patterns of behaviour are handed down from father to son, and usually accepted without question. Only in few societies—fifth-century Greece, for instance, and perhaps our own—has there been a general questioning of the currently accepted morality. For the rest, men have been content to accept the ways of their fathers, either without justification or without stopping to consider whether the justification conventionally offered was sound. The truth is, men are conformist, and it is much less difficult to inculcate moral standards than is commonly supposed.

The love of God is thus not the only foundation on which morality can be built. Other foundations have been used, with fair success, and for the most part morality can be propagated without any rational justification being put forward at all. Yet the love of God, I say, is the only really adequate foundation. Other foundations can be used for a time, and very imposing systems can be built on them: but with the passage of time the logic of their own position asserts itself, and the morality is eroded. In the Middle Ages the popular morality was largely founded on the hope of heaven and the fear of hell. These were powerful inducements to good behaviour, but in the end proved powerful inducements also to the purchase of indulgences. The doctrine of predestination as developed by Calvin imbued those who felt within themselves the working of God's grace with great power and determination to carry out their part of the divine plan: but it also decided others, who believed themselves condemned to everlasting pains and torments in the world to come, to enjoy what pleasures they could in this life at any rate, and even perhaps to do something to justify the sentence they could not escape; and it has also led people in our own time to disbelieve in this God, who had been represented as more to be feared than respected, and more worthy of hate than of love. In similar fashion, the justification of honesty as being the best policy, was highly effective in the mercantile society of the eighteenth and nineteenth centuries, but has taken some hard knocks in our own age of motivation research and high pressure advertising. Other examples abound. One way of looking at history, though not a fashionable one, is to see it as tracing the development and growth and final decay of different ideas of morality with their different, though always inadequate, justifications of morality. A great part of the history of man is the history of his ideologies, or as the Christian would term them, his idolatries. Man is a natural idolater. He has always been willing, even anxious, to worship other gods than God, gods, which being limited make only limited demands on him. He has found such gods, and has used them to his own satisfaction. But in the course of centuries, and under the rain of countless selfish assessments and selfish approaches, these other gods have been found in the end to have feet of clay.

The propagation of morality without a supporting ideology also fails in the long run, though in a different way. It is not distorted, as moralities supported by an inadequate justification are: rather, it ossifies and goes dead. The best case is that of Jewish society of Our Lord's own time. After the traumatic experience of the exile, Judah gave up idolatry for good. They never again went a-whoring after strange gods, but clung to the Mosaic Law with a fanatical tenacity which has earned them ever since the admiration and the hatred of the gentile world. Precept upon precept, proverb upon proverb, psalm upon psalm hammered home to the Jewish youth the necessity of obeying, of observing every detail of the Law. The Law became more and more elaborate. There were no new insights. Prophets were no more popular than in the time of Ahab, and were more effectively suppressed. The result was a religion of obedience with a very high and exacting moral standard, but one in which all sense of joy and spontaneity had been lost. Morality which is merely conventional morality always has this effect. It inhibits personality because it is itself no more than a set of instilled inhibitions. Our own time, as well as that of Jesus, abounds with people who are utterly conventional, who have been moulded into a standard pattern and can only produce stock responses.

It is not that the code of morality is itself at fault. The Mosaic code, particularly in its revised form in the book of Deuteronomy, was a very good code, infused with the spirit of love, and with many touches of humanity, and the present-day code of the conventional moralist is, as moral codes go, liberal and humane. What is wrong in each case is not the content of the code, but the fact that it is a code and accepted *merely* as such. The respectable behaviour of the conventionally good man is the result of a passive acquiescence in externally promulgated norms, not the active adoption of them as outlining a way of life which he wants to make his own. Merely to observe the letter of the law—even if it was originally a law of love—killeth: it destroys the personality, and replaces it by a stereotyped impersonality. Only the spirit can make alive; and that, if endorsed and made one's own, restores the personality and altogether revivifies and renews it. Christian morality has a regenerative power that other moralities lack. Although other moralities have much greater capacity for surviving than is commonly allowed, so that it is false to claim that belief in the Christian God is the only possible foundation for morality, they survive only at the cost of either becoming less and less moral as they are handed on from generation to generation or of losing their inwardness. They become either counsels of prudence, telling people how to achieve certain ends, or externally imposed conventions. Sooner or later, though it may be later rather than sooner, it will become apparent that what purports to be morality is either a scheme for self-advancement or a dead hush of meaningless taboos; and sooner or later, is spite of the very great readiness of children to take over their parents' moral standards without examination, moralities which are wrongly justified or are passed on without any justification whatsoever will lose their grip and will be rejected as not being moralities at all. Only Christian morality will endure from one generation to another, because it alone will be re-authenticated and re-affirmed in each generation, as soul by soul men are touched by the love of God, and come in their turn to love God with all their heart and mind and soul and strength.

A man who has known the love of God towards him will in return himself love God, and God's children also. This is the reason for his doing the many things that he ought to do. Just as the natural affections of humanity, man for woman, parent for child, child for parent, brother for brother, and friend for friend, engender certain types of behaviour, so the Christian's conduct towards God and towards all men is, so far as he can make it, the vehicle of his love. But he cannot make it very far. The Christian knows himself not only to be finite but to be fallible; and all considerations of Christian conduct are coloured by a realization of the ineradicable imperfection of humanity. This is why Christianity, in spite of its deep suspicion of moral codes and its acute insight into the spiritual diseases to which moral man is subject, does not dispense with 'U-type' morality altogether, and have solely an 'E-type' morality of personal commitment to the person of Christ and the way of love.[1] Set against the Christian's understanding of God is his understanding of man: the divine love that is capable of moving all things, and is the only good motive for being good that there is, is distorted in its action through the agency of selfish and stupid men, who are far from necessarily loving the highest when they see it, and who only occasionally and fitfully respond to God's call and see what they ought to do and do it.

It is unfortunately easy to be eloquent about sin, and Christian thinkers from St Paul and St Augustine downwards have used language which while expressing their feelings very well has not made for clarity of understanding. Much as a lover is overcome

---

[1] The distinction between U- and E-types of morality is due to E. A. Gellner, 'Ethics and Logic', *Proceedings of the Aristotelian Society*, LV (1954–5), pp. 157–8; for a further development, see P. F. Strawson, 'Social Morality and Individual Ideal', *Philosophy*, XXXVI (1961), pp. 1–17.

with a sense of his own unworthiness of the love of his beloved, so the Christian, as he approaches God and begins to appreciate the fullness of God's love towards him, is filled with a realization of how little he deserves such love, and how nothing he has done merits so boundless a return. But this is a truth about love, not about man. Love never can be deserved, or extorted or expected as the merited reward for one's own goodness. Gratitude can be deserved, respect can be deserved, but love to be love must always be given freely, must always flow forth without consideration of the merits of the beloved. God loves us not for anything we have done, but because we are his children. And as we come to know his love, we come also to know how little we deserve it. And it is very easy to express this by making ourselves out to be not merely unworthy of God's love, which we must of conceptual necessity be, but altogether worthless and wicked, which in the common way of speaking is often false. St Paul and St Augustine were not monsters of depravity, in the way that Nero or Heliogabalus were. They were good men. Most of the men we know and come across in our daily life are good men, not good in comparison with God, not good enough to deserve the love God manifests towards them, but good all the same and better than they might be. It is true, and needs to be emphasized, because men are everlastingly apt to forget it, that to be good as men go is not good enough. At the end of it all we remain unprofitable servants. But there are degrees of unprofitableness, and God, who is so much concerned with what actually happens in this world that he came into it in the form of a human being, is concerned with what we do, and it does matter that we should do one thing, inadequate though that is, rather than another. The rich ruler, who had kept the moral law from his youth up, lacked something still: but deficient though he was, he was far less deficient than if he had not kept the commandments, if he had, as other rulers have done, committed murder, robbery, and adultery upon his unfortunate subjects. Hitler was a wicked and bad man in the way that the rich ruler was not; and God cares enough for this world and the sufferings of humanity not to obliterate the distinction by condemning both equally as being totally depraved. And for our part, too, if we are to think clearly about Christian morality, we must take care not to confuse the truth that no man is good enough to merit the love of God with the falsehood that no man is ever good at all.

The Christian doctrine of sin, therefore, is very different from what the popular connotation of the word suggests. It has very little to do with sex, and not much to do with behaviour. It is much more to do with one's attitude of mind—whether one is fundamentally self-centred or not—and with personal relationships—one's personal relationship with God. The immediate bearing the doctrine has on the problem of deciding what one should do, is that men are fallible. Even when we are most sure that we are right, we may be wrong. This is not to say that we always are wrong—man is made in God's image, and it would be a poor likeness which matched the absolute rightness of God with an absolute wrongness in man. Far from always being wrong, we believe that, thanks to the reason and common sense with which God has endowed us, men are able to discover what is right, and quite often do. In the last resort we often have to trust our own judgement, because we have no other resource, and when we do so, we should do so with courage; but also with humility. However sure we are that we are right, we must not arrogate to ourselves an infallibility that is God's alone. People who are religious are peculiarly liable to the vice of talking a lot about humility but excepting from its application the way in which they hold their own beliefs. Our thinking ought to be as humble as our doing. We often have to make up our minds, and sometimes we may be reasonably confident that we have done so rightly, but always we should go delicately before our God, the more so when we are acting, as we think, at his behest or on his behalf.

Not only does the fallibility of human judgement affect the degree of certitude we ought to have in our moral convictions, but together with the finiteness of human beings, it affects their content also. First, we *need* to be educated morally. We do not naturally develop a flair for always doing the right thing. Although it is false to maintain that the moral judgement is merely the result of instilled inhibitions, it is also false to believe that each man will, of his own accord and without help from outside, develop a right judgement in morals or anything else. Children do not learn to behave, any more than they learn to speak, without the example and the precepts of adults. It is partly a matter of instruction, partly a matter of drawing out latent sympathies already there. But often we need to give the lessons before the child is old enough to appreciate it all for himself. Just as we, quite rightly, teach children poetry, poetry about love for example, before they can have the experience which makes it come alive, in order that when the time comes they may be already equipped with the concepts with which to articulate, and indeed even to have, the experience; so we, quite rightly, inculcate patterns of behaviour first, in order that in due course they can appreciate what the moral principle is that they are being urged to adopt. The concept of gratitude is more the effect than the cause of the habit of saying 'Thank you', and a child needs first to be checked in his natural mendacity before he can comprehend what talk of truthfulness is about. Nor is it only children who have to be told. We go on needing to be told—if only by ourselves—throughout our lives. We cannot live a life of complete spontaneity, not even as adults, because our feelings are too fickle. One minute I may be filled with love and benevolence to a colleague or a child; the next minute the colleague crosses me, or the child breaks something, and my natural reaction is one of anger. If I am to achieve the goals I set myself in my moments of love, I must discipline myself not to give way to my feelings in my periods of non-love. So variable are my whims that if I am to do what I want to do I must be prepared to do what I often do not want to do.

We thus have to reduce the extreme complexity of the Christian life of love to relatively few principles, in much the same way as we have to reduce the complexity of English (or Latin or any other language) composition to a few grammatical and syntactical principles when we want to teach someone. We need the moral law in something of the same way as we need grammar books. We formulate schematized and condensed sets of rules, because these can be taught to pupils fairly readily, and only when the pupil has mastered these can he develop the finer points of style. And just as we are careful to point out that to write grammatical English is not to have a good English style, so we also insist that to keep the commandments is not to live the Christian life. A man can keep all the rules of grammar, and yet write woodenly, and a man can keep the whole of the moral law and yet live a deadly life.

The comparison between moral rules and rules of grammar, although illuminating, does not exhaust our account of U-type morality in Christianity. We need moral rules not only because of the frailty of our judgement, but because of the finitude of our information. If we had complete knowledge of situations then

—conceivably—we might do as Christ would have done; but we always have only partial knowledge, often very limited knowledge indeed. I do not know, when accosted by a beggar, whether he is an unfortunate man down on his luck, or an unscrupulous one hoping to cadge the price of a drink. Christ knew exactly when to be gentle and when to be rough: when to heal lepers and when to whip money-changers. I do not know, and must be guided much more by rules of thumb. I can take only a finite number of factors into consideration. My rules of thumb can be at best only crude approximations of God's unerring touch. I cannot hope to do always exactly the right thing; the most I can hope for is not ever to be too far from the mark, and to remain always ready to revise my judgement in the light of fuller knowledge or fuller understanding. Finitude involves my acting in according with rules: for I cannot have antecedently drawn relevant distinctions between every situation I may meet, or I should need an infinite number of distinctions; and so I can specify in a finite number of words only the type of situation to which a certain type of response is appropriate. On the other hand, fallibility requires that these rules always are only *prima facie* rules, because however fully we have specified any one of them, further knowledge or further understanding may always reveal a further relevant factor, which affects whether or not the rule as initially stated is applicable or not.

There is a third facet of human sinfulness on account of which we have to have moral rules: this is our imperfect disavowal of self and the imperfect commitment to God not only of ourselves but of others also. The ideal of love is one of complete self-giving; and the practice is one of only partial self-giving. In view of this, the ideal of Christian behaviour is not practicable; and Christian morals are concerned with practice—what shall I do? No point in Christian moral philosophy causes greater difficulty than this. Christianity is both an intensely idealistic and an intensely realistic religion. Christ had no illusions about the men he was coming to save, and it is part of the Christian's duty to make ruthlessly realistic assessments about man in general and himself in particular. There is no virtue in loving sinners by pretending that they are not sinners. They are. And we must love them all the same. Although sometimes being loved will transform the sinner, it will not always. Men sometimes remain obdurate in their ways, and any programme of Christian conduct must take this into account. The ideal remains that we should all live together in brotherly love and amity; the reality remains that we shall not, but shall always be to a greater or less extent self-centred and selfish; some more, some less, but none not at all, save only our Saviour, Jesus Christ.

Moral codes, like legal codes with their careful distribution of rights and duties, accept and legitimate the notion of the self. We learn '*Suum cuique*', and 'Do not do to others what you would not have done to yourself'. Although the excesses of self-will are curbed, the self remains. Therein lies the weakness of the moral law, as we have seen, but also its strength. The moral law is something I can set myself to keep; and, indeed, so strong is the *nisus* towards ego-centricity in man, that whatever I set myself to keep, I shall begin to regard that as a sort of legalistic code, in which I, number one, play a crucial part. This is an attitude we keep falling back into. We do not live by it always, but we never succeed in living by it not at all. The attitude of mind that Christ sketched in the Sermon on the Mount and throughout the Gospels we do succeed in cultivating a certain amount—but only within limits. And when these limits are exceeded we fall back onto some moral code. According to St Matthew's account, Christ recognizes this, and outlines the procedure for the Christian to deal with wrongs against himself:[1] first have a word with the man concerned in private; if that is no good, have it out with him in the presence of witnesses; if that fails, make a public issue of it; and if the wrongdoer remains recalcitrant still, then sever personal relations with him altogether. Christianity is not, as is popularly supposed, simply a matter of turning the other cheek. To think this, and generally to construe the Sermon on the Mount as a new and more stringent code of behaviour, replacing that of the Mosaic Law, is to misunderstand it altogether. For it would still be a code, with the added disadvantage of being an impracticable one; and any one who tries to live by it as a code is not only missing the central point of Christ's teaching about conduct, that it is the attitude rather than the actual actions by themselves that count, but is also committing himself to a life of intellectual dishonesty if he pretends that he, a sinner living among sinners, is really going to follow the Sermon on the Mount *au pied de la lettre*.

[1] Matt. 18. 15–17; some scholars see these rules as not really our Lord's own, but rather those of the early Church.

13 THE CHURCH AND SECULAR SOCIETY

Christians often complain about the Church. The buildings may have merit as architectural monuments: the regular services as exercises in quaint liturgical prose: and the occasional offices as a socially decorous way of celebrating births and marriages and of paying respect to the dead. But it seems a far cry from Christ's band of companions in Galilee, or the Church of the apostles after Pentecost, and we yearn for something more real, more alive, more relevant, than the young people's club on Tuesdays at 6.45 and the Mothers' Union celebration on Thursdays at 11. The Church, we say, should be a worshipping community. It is quite wrong that we should meet only on Sundays, and then barely pass the time of day as we hasten home to Sunday lunch: we ought to work together as well as pray together, and our faith should find expression in our workaday lives, and not merely as a leisure activity in the evenings or at weekends.

If we follow this line of argument through, we are led to a new monasticism. Christians should separate themselves out from the secular world, and live the whole of their lives in a Christian context, living and working in communities which can give corporate expression to their common faith in our Lord. I think there is a place in the universal Church for such communities; not only of the traditional monastic type, but looser organizations not restricted to celibates, and perhaps not practising common ownership of material goods in its entirety. Many people feel the need, especially in the amorphous and anonymous conurbations of the West, for smaller and more meaningful forms of social life; and it may be a vocation of the Church, borrowing once again from the Jews, to cater for this need by the foundation of Christian kibbutzim, some of them setting out to serve mankind in providing housing, or medical psychiatric or welfare services, in the same sort of way that the traditional monastic orders have in time past.

But monasticism has never been, and most certainly is not now, the sole or main vocation of the Church. Some Christians are called to the monastic life, but most are not. Nor this because they are second-class Christians, not up to the highest levels of Christian performance. Our Lord was made flesh, and dwelt among us, going to weddings and parties, paying taxes and talking to friends, as well as preaching the gospel, and occasionally going to the Temple; and we do well to follow his example, living in the world, sharing its concerns, its pleasures and sorrows, as well as witnessing to the faith and going to church. Indeed, just as God could tell us the Good News by becoming human and living in our world, so the Church cannot preach the gospel effectively unless it does likewise. Great though the services of the teaching and medical orders have been, the fact that they are orders, living under a rule and separated from ordinary men and women, has been a barrier to their message getting through everywhere. The Church, as well as rendering many specialized services to mankind, needs also to serve in the unspecialized way of sharing in men's ordinary life and ordinary concerns; and if the Church is fully to penetrate the world, it can only be by individual Christians living and working in the world, and manifesting the love of God in innumerable, often humdrum or trivial, ways, as occasion arises.

Once we accept the Church's secular function in society, many of its difficulties and frustrations can be seen as the inevitable concomitant of the role it is called upon to play. If most Christians are going to work in the world, specifically churchy activities are going to be confined to leisure time. They are none the worse for that. On Sunday mornings the congregation is offering up not bread and wine simply, but as representing all the work that has been done in the previous week. The youth clubs and the social gatherings *are* peripheral to most people's main interests—but none the worse for that; so are staff parties, race-meetings, and miners' Gala Days—peripheral, but of great significance to the texture of their lives. Clergymen often are acting as under-paid civil servants in marrying and burying people—but although a less heroic role than that of the Suffering Servant, it is not an ignoble one. Churches often seem empty mausoleums rather than houses of prayer; but Jesus continued to go to the Temple in spite of the emptiness of its worship, and we are not failing him in cherishing our church buildings as he did his. They are not the centre of the Christian religion, any more than youth clubs or Mothers' Unions are: but Christianity does not have a centre that can be neatly encompassed, encapsulated and put in a nutshell. It spills over everywhere, and for most Christians most of their Christianity will be expressed in activities which are carried on in the colloquial sense of the word outside the Church. This means that the Church is largely left with the left-overs, which do not seem very exciting or significant. Feetwashing never is.

14 THE OTHER FACE OF PERMISSIVENESS

The permissive society is often argued for on grounds of liberty and equality. Each man should be free to make his own choices, so long as they do not cause harm to another, and each man's choices are equally valid. Society ought not to put pressure on people to choose one way rather than another, either because it is no business of the public how private individuals exercise their freedom or because no rational difference can subsist between one choice and another. Either way we should forbear to criticize, and let people make up their own minds for themselves.

The argument is attractive, but goes too far. Freedom is important, and there are often good reasons for minding our own business and not concerning ourselves with how other people manage their affairs. And when it comes to value-judgements there is an important principle of equality, that nobody's opinion can be ruled out of court merely on account of the way it is stated or the person who propounds it. In mathematics and the natural sciences there are decision-procedures which conclusively refute certain positions, and in law and politics certain people lack an authority that others possess. Not so in morals—every opinion is entitled to a fair trial, and in this sense there is an equality before the law, with each man's opinions having an equal *prima facie* right to be heard. But that is all. It does not follow that each man's opinion, having been heard, must be adjudged equally correct, any more than equality before the law requires that the judge must find equally in favour of the two sides of the case. The whole exercise would be pointless if he was not going to decide for one side rather than the other, and the whole point of rival value-judgements is that each is laying claim to the hearer's acceptance, and we cannot accept both. If once we take the view of them *de gustibus non disputandum*, they cease to be value-judgements in our eyes; and *per contra*, if they are value-judgements they are arguable about, and cannot be regarded as being all of equal validity. Even so, however, there are often good reasons for leaving people free to reach their own conclusions and to act on them; and especially for not employing the coercive machinery of the state to enforce conformity. But this cannot be an absolute freedom. Even extreme liberals allow the need to curtail one man's liberty to save another from harm; and since 'harm' is a very elastic concept, this exception is a very large one. But I think there is a more fundamental argument still against permissiveness.

Permissiveness is two-way. If you are to be allowed to do exactly what you like without interference from me, I must be allowed to do exactly what I like without complaint from you. In particular, if I do not like the way you exercise your freedom, I am free to have nothing to do with you. If you are free to act in ways I very much dislike, I must be free to have no lot or part in your activities, and to exclude you and all your works from my private world. For we do take note of one another's opinions and actions, if not in public life, certainly in our private and social life. I associate with my friends because I like doing things with them and share the same interests. If I do not care what a person thinks or does, it means that he is nothing to me, and is no friend of mine. If no other sanction may be used against those who exercise their freedom in profoundly repugnant ways, the sanction of non-association is still available. And it will be used. Although on some issues, on which people do not feel all that strongly, they may be prepared to swallow their principles, and continue to consort with those who blatantly flout them, they are not prepared to compromise their integrity indefinitely. Left-wing radicals are not prepared to associate themselves with racialists. And if it were the law that racialists were entitled to hold and act upon their own opinions without let or hindrance, the only response open to anti-racialists would be to boycott them. People with like opinions would consort together—as they do—and would form coteries and cliques from which every one else would be excluded. This at present does not happen, because we do not believe in the permissive society, and can therefore admit people to our fellowship without being debarred from criticizing their opinions or bringing pressure on them to alter their ways. But if the permissive premiss were accepted, argument would be impossible, and we should merely go our separate ways.

Contemporary permissiveness is largely concerned with sex. But not everyone agrees that promiscuity is a good thing, and those who are unwilling to cheapen sex are not going to want their children to be brought up to treat it casually, and will seek to exclude from their circle those whom they regard as menaces to family life. Only certain people will be acceptable in certain circles. Extreme social exclusiveness will flourish in an atmosphere of official permissiveness. I believe this happened in America in the late nineteenth and early twentieth centuries. All men were free and equal in the eyes of the law, and entitled to pursue happiness as they pleased—but high society in many towns was more select and more strictly guarded than anything we have known in England, where we do not believe that one should pursue happiness by never letting anyone darken the door of one's house unless he is a member of one's own charmed circle. And we can reasonably expect people not to be too exclusive, and to open their doors a little, so long as they can do so on the basis of some shared morality, and can believe that, subject to many qualifications and practical provisos, it is a matter of public concern how a man exercises his freedom of choice. That is enough to provide the basis for a general sense of community between different members of society, and to provide some reason against society breaking up into a number of cliques and coteries. Otherwise, granted that people have some privacy and some freedom, and in view of the fact that we cannot but care how our associates behave, the only effect of permissiveness will be to enthrone snobbery. Permissiveness and *apartheid* are two sides of the same coin.

15 THE EUCHARIST

A sermon preached before the University of Oxford on Sunday 7th November 1971

I take my text from Iris Murdoch, towards the end of her novel, *The Bell.* 'But what did, from his former life, remain to him was the Mass. . . . The Mass remained, not consoling, not uplifting, but in some way factual. . . . It simply existed as a kind of pure reality separate from the weaving of his own thoughts' (p. 309 Penguin), where the hero, Michael, is losing all faith in God, and is finding that nothing matters very much.

But the Mass remains, in some way factual; it exists, as a kind of pure reality. *In some way* factual, as a *kind of* pure reality. Iris Murdoch is very cautious in qualifying her words. Christians have found it extraordinarily difficult to devise words to say what they want to say about their rite. Although the holy Eucharist has been, to outside observers, the most distinctive characteristic of the Christian religion from Pliny the Younger until Miss Murdoch, and to those within its fellowship, the most central and sustaining part of the Christian life: yet it has also been a chief cause of dissension and focus of disunity between the warring sects of Christ's divided body. The reason why many loyal Anglicans today cannot welcome union with our fellow-Christians in the Methodist Church is that they do not believe the Lord's Supper can be celebrated except by a priest episcopally ordained in the Apostolic Succession. The reason why we cannot kneel at the same altar as our fellow-Christians in the Church of Rome is that they are obliged to talk of a sacrifice in terms which do not ring entirely true to Anglican ears, and believe that God's presence can best be expressed by the doctrine of transubstantiation, whereas we hold, in the words of the Thirty-Nine Articles that transubstantiation 'cannot be proved by Holy Writ, is repugnant to the plain words of Scripture, overthroweth the nature of a Sacrament, and hath given occasion to many superstitions'.

Few Roman Catholics would deny that there have been superstitious practices associated with the blessed Sacrament: but if they were to enquire what alternative doctrine the Church of England had to put forward, they could justly complain that although we are very clear about what we do not believe, we are

109

cautious to the point of obscurity about what we do believe. For the most part we have been content to echo Queen Elizabeth I:

'Twas God the word that spake it,
He took the bread and brake it,
And what the word did make it
That I believe, and take it.

The attitude of the Church of England has been one of loyalty rather than belief. We have gone to the Early Service because Christ told us to, and we think we ought to do his bidding in ritual liturgy, as well as workaday life. It has been a service, a *leitourgia* more than anything else, with a corresponding unclarity about how else what we were doing was to be described. For the last four centuries our eucharistic theology has been 'if not transubstantiation then what?'

I do not think we have been entirely wrong to be so uncertain in our belief. The Holy Spirit has been guiding us into this region of truth by not letting us accept good answers to bad questions, in order that we might ultimately learn not to ask those questions but attempt to frame better. And although all our questions will be too crude, and all the analogies inadequate, which I shall draw from the homely, if not particularly humble, circumstances of our Oxford life, yet I think we ought to ask fresh questions, even at the risk of giving wrong answers, both as a working out of the doctrine of the incarnation, and as an escape from the frozen attitudes of ancient quarrels, which often have rested on assumptions we ought not to have made. *If* the question is asked whether the Mass is factual or not, there is a profound truth in saying that it is in some way factual. But merely to ask this question is to beg many others. Facts are not the simple things plain men take them to be, nor are they at all worthy to be worshipped. Reality is even more misleading. If any one asks us, we cannot deny the reality of the Mass or that there is a Real Presence of God at the Eucharist. Not even the most extreme Protestant professes a doctrine of the Real Absence. But the word 'real' was made up by the philosophers from *res*, a thing, and has never lost its thingly overtones. Things not only exist in their own right independently of us, but also are what we can manipulate for our own purposes. In their attempt to assure us that God was indeed with us at the Holy Communion, and not merely that we had subjective impressions of his presence then, the Schoolmen made out the consecrated elements to be so thing-like that they could be carted around and exposed, like talismans or secret weapons, at the time of battle. In talking about God we are constantly needing to use, and are constantly tempted to misuse, the language of things. God, like a thing, is independent of us, stable and reliable, a Rock which endures from one generation to another, on which we can stand and in which we can shelter. But God, unlike a thing, can never be merely used, because he is a person and more than any of our contrivings can control.

If we, as theists, believe that the universe is fundamentally personal in character, it follows that our ultimate understanding will not be in terms of things, which occupy space and may or may not possess certain properties, but of persons, who characteristically *do* things. Action, not substance, will be our most important category of thought. It is a truth too long neglected by philosophers. Since the time of Descartes, philosophers have taken a very inactive view of the mind, and have shut themselves up in their rooms, cogitating hard and wondering whether they have a sufficiently clear and distinct idea of the external world to be justified in believing that it exists. But we do not learn much about either ourselves or the world, unless we abandon inactivity, and try and do things. We learn by trial and error, failure and success; and our starting-point for understanding our own essential nature should be not *cogito, ergo sum* as Descartes thought, but rather *ego, ergo ago*, I, therefore I act. Christians are bidden to be doers of the word and not cogitators only. Action has the further, logical advantage in being a much less exclusive category than substance. An action can be correctly described in many different ways, as raising one's arms, shaking somebody else's hand, making up a quarrel, and carrying out a Christian duty. These descriptions do not exclude one another, in the way that if we describe a substance as pure sodium chloride we exclude the possibility of its being also described as calcium carbonate. And so, too, the Eucharist, if we regard it as an *action*, can be described in many different ways without their being inherently incompatible with one another. If we say that we are making a memorial of Christ's most precious death, we are not thereby precluded from saying also that the minister, as *alter Christus* is presiding at the heavenly banquet, or that the priest, on behalf of the whole Church, is offering up the sacrifice of the Mass.

Actions are non-exclusive in another way, too. The fact that an action is *mine* does not prevent it from being *yours* also, as when you ask me to do something for you. We say that Solomon built the Temple, or that William of Wykeham built Winchester, but do not mean to deny the labours of the many masons and craftsmen who fashioned the stones, and laid them one upon the other. They also built the Temple, they also built Winchester. A man often acts through the willing co-operation of the others, and can be with them responsible for what is done. And so, too, what is done in church not only can be described in many ways, but can be said to be done by *many*, and sometimes *different*, people—by the congregation, by the priest, by the visible Church militant here on earth, by the whole Church, by Christ on the same night as he was betrayed, by Christ now, risen, ascended, and in glory.

In the Church of England the dominant understanding of the Eucharist has been in terms of *doing*, a simple doing in obedience to our Lord's command, a service, the Early Service, to which, in George Orwell's picture of England, old maids would bike through the mists of the autumn mornings. 'Do this . . .', he told us, and therefore we do it, beseeching God, in the words of the Prayer Book, 'to accept this our bounden duty and service', and in the uglier but more emphatic words of Series 3 '. . . as we follow his example and obey his command. . . . Therefore, O heavenly Father, we do this . . . .' And since we are doing this at Christ's command, he is doing it too. We are building up the life of the Church, and through our actions, the intentions of the Founder of Christianity are being put into effect, as those of other founders and master-builders have been. Even by the most secular of reckonings Jesus started something when he took the bread and wine, and shared it round. And a large part of what we feel as we go to church each Sunday is that we are fellow-workers with Christ, in carrying out his injunctions, as we and our predecessors have done Sunday by Sunday, in a continuous succession, every single week, since Thursday, 6th April, A.D. 30, or whenever it was that the Last Supper actually took place.

The Eucharist is a doing, but it is not only that. Although it has been a merit of many loyal laymen in the Church of England to stress the note of simple obedience, it has also been a defect, in that it has played down the special characteristics of the Eucharist, and its place in the Christian life. If the Early Service is seen just as *a* service of the Church, there are other services equally suitable to be rendered to the Lord as well as many secular duties we believe we ought to discharge in accordance with his will. We do not obey well if we obey blindly, and if we are to do this in remembrance of him, we must think afresh and try to understand what it is that we are doing. Let us therefore return with Iris Murdoch and observe a celebration, as it were, from the outside. Undoubtedly it is an activity, a social activity, not a manufacturing process. People are saying things, sometimes to one another, sometimes together. Something is being eaten, something drunk. Something is being given, and something given back, and the proceedings evidently mean something very significant to all concerned. These bare descriptions, not only *doing*, but *doing together, saying, eating, drinking, giving, being given back, meaning*, are the strands which our Lord, and, at his bidding, the Church, have woven together in instituting the Eucharist. We cannot expound it as being merely an action, a corporate activity, a teach-in, a common meal, an offertory, a reception, or a symbolic rite, for it is more than all these. Nevertheless, it is these. These were features of the Last Supper, as they had been of the Passover in ancient Israel, which enabled it to be what our Lord intended it to be, and it is these features that have enabled the Eucharist to be the focus of the Church's corporate life on earth and the main way whereby the individual Christian can enter into a relationship with God.

The Last Supper was a meal. The sharing of a meal is the most fundamental sort of sharing for human beings. Many other values may be cherished by many men in common—a love of England, or of medieval architecture or of mathematical logic: but not everyone loves England or medieval architecture or mathematical logic, and any corporate activity centred on these as their focus of common concern would necessarily be selective and exclusive. But we all know that we need food and drink, and therefore all value food and drink. To offer a man a morsel or to give him a drink is a gesture that cannot but be taken as a token of good will; and to join in eating and drinking is to engage in a common activity which each man, however individualistic his standpoint, must regard as desirable and good. And although it is possible to satisfy

113

one's bodily hunger in isolation, it is in another sense very un-satisfying to do so, and the solitary eater, like the solitary drinker, is an object of pity and compassion. Wherever possible we eat and drink in company, and only in company is either really satisfying.

We can understand the Eucharist in part as the fellowship meal of the Church. Christians draw round the common table of the Church for much the same reasons and in something of the same spirit as members of a college dine together in Hall. It both expresses and helps to build up a sense of community and a feeling of fellowship, a recognition that because we cherish certain values in common therefore we want to maintain together a common life. Indeed, even when we are drawn together by a shared sorrow, we still find it appropriate to express our fellow-feeling by also eating and drinking together. The Last Supper was the funeral bakemeats for our Lord's death, and the weekly Eucharist parallels in part the 'year's mind', when we remember the departed, and in our sadness also rejoice. On such occasions it is natural and correct to ascribe the activity of those present to the influence of the deceased, and even to say that he brought about the things that they do. Merton College owes its existence to Walter of Merton and would not have existed but for him, and has at least to some extent been the embodiment of his spirit. We also go further and say, more metaphorically, that the dead man still lives in the memory and activity of his friends, or the teacher in the minds of his pupils, or the founder in his foundation. This is not to claim immortality. Rather, it is once again to view human beings as primarily agents, and therefore to say that they are what they do, and hence also what they achieve through the agency of other men's actions. The spirit of Socrates lives in the intellectual friendship and philosophical discussions of his disciples, especial-ly when they are all gathered together in his name, and doing the things he wanted them to do and had in his own time done himself. And so too the Christians, when they express their cor-porate solidarity by eating and drinking together, may also remember their master, and feel that he still lives in their common life.

But it is a very thin life. Jeremy Bentham hoped that the young men of University College, London, would continue to be con-vivial after his death and spare a kindly thought for him, but added the further provision that his corpse, which was to be embalmed and kept in University College, should attend these parties, so that he might be present in the flesh. It is a macabre idea, but expresses the sense of inadequacy of being there merely in spirit. If the Lord's Supper were merely a fellowship meal in which Christians looked back to the passion and remembered Jesus Christ, it would be similarly inadequate: but the Lord's Supper is not merely a get-together of like-minded friends, because the Last Supper was not merely that. The disciples were not merely dining together, they were dining with God. And the Lord's Supper is not merely a commemoration dinner which we eat with other Christians to commemorate our departed Lord; it is also the Lord's because, in the light of the resurrection, he is present and we are dining with him at his high table, as we look forward to the future and not only back to the past. It is the Lord Mayor's banquet, with the Lord Mayor present, and everyone celebrating his accession to power.

The future is very different from the past. We can keep on commemorating the same event, but we cannot keep on inaugurating the same era. I can only once come of age, a wedding can only once be celebrated, and the second coming, when it comes, will come only once. It follows that the celebration of the Eucharist which we, in accordance with our Lord's command, repeat day by day or week by week, cannot be exactly the inaugural banquet of Christ's accession. We can, in part, see in the Eucharist a foretaste of a greater banquet yet to come: we can liken it to the Queen's Accession service, a thanksgiving for Christ's triumph, which is still, and will continue to be, effective in our lives; but in order to get the full force of the immediate forward-looking aspect of the Eucharist we have to make a slightly sophisticated change of reference. Rather than think of it as the Lord Mayor's banquet, given by a particular Lord Mayor, we need to compare it with a more generalized celebration of inauguration. In our culture we should compare it with New Year parties. These can be repeated, and yet are indisputably oriented towards the future. As we see the New Year in, we do not suppose that 1972 will be an entirely new sort of existence in contrast to 1971: our celebration is not tied to the particularity of the year, but to the generality of the newness. And in the Eucharist we celebrate the fact that we are granted newness of life, not merely as a matter of secular fact, but in the life of the Spirit. Thanks to Christ's death and resurrection, we can go forward in confidence and look to the future in hope. A new possibility having been opened for us by Christ, we are realizing it for ourselves every time we share the Lord's Supper with the brethren, and *ta men opiso epilanthanomenoi tois de emprosthen epekteinometha* (cf. Phil. 3. 13b), forgetting what is behind, reach out to that which lies ahead. The Eucharist is not merely a memorial of things long past, but is the expression of a doctrine of *epectasis*, and an effective implementation of it in our lives, a weekly New Day's party to celebrate the fact that by virtue of the resurrection we shall always be finding new things to do, new things worth doing, new ways of making each his own contribution, new treasures still of countless price, new thoughts of God, new hopes of heaven. Not only *illic*, as Peter Abelard said, but equally

> *hic ex sabbato succedit sabbatum*
> *perpes laetitia sabbatizantium.*

Although the Last Supper was a supper, and some of the earliest celebrations of the Eucharist may have been real meals, there was from New Testament times onwards a tendency to whittle down the meal to a purely symbolic form. Some of the reasons were practical. In addition to those of decorum given by St Paul, a real meal is relatively costly, and the early Church did not have the odd two hundred denarii available to ensure that all should be filled. Banquets, although real, tend to be expensive and exclusive. If the poor are to be able to be filled with the good things from the Lord's Table, only nominal amounts of bread and wine can be handed out, which must act as tokens of what is being given us. But this attenuation of the Supper to the Eucharist both requires and automatically heightens a symbolic interpretation. Just because we are not getting very much to eat and drink, we are impelled to understand what we are doing as not being merely eating and drinking. This is a tension between different requirements. Unless the Lord's Supper is celebrated by our really eating food and really imbibing drink, we lose the basic principle that it is a good thing for everyone who joins in: but unless we are prepared to sit loose to the satisfaction of our bodily hunger and thirst we may lose sight of the principle that it is something more than merely physical satisfaction.

In the Eucharist, especially in the congregational liturgies of

England and America, we give, and are given. It is a natural instinct, and a very familiar one here in Oxford, where every don likes to make a contribution to his own subject. The harvest festival motif is powerful even in our own unspiritual age. It is natural, especially for laymen, whose vocation is to serve God by means of mundane activities in the secular world, to offer their work to God, not only to give thanks for material benefits, but because, especially in the modern world, only if we are sent out into the world in the power of his Spirit, can the tedium of everyday work be made endurable. After a week of repetition work at Cowley, or even of tutorials that are sometimes somewhat stodgy and of committee meetings that are less than totally inspiring, we offer our work to God, and ask him to make it his because only so can it be worth doing and supportable. It is right to understand the Eucharist as a giving. But giving is peculiarly liable to the corruption of the human heart. It easily degenerates into trading or expands into presumption. If we are lawyers we may start thinking of the offertory as a *quid pro quo*, or like Cyprian, as a sort of court fee that has to be paid for the right of audience with the Almighty. And even where there is no element of payment, we may hesitate to assume that we are so much on a level with God that we can send him presents, and may say with David (1 Chron. 29. 14) 'What am I, and what is my people, that we should be able to give willingly like this?' And hence many Christians have come to think that only God can be offered to God, since only Christ can speak for us in the heavenly places. But although we can see why people have been led to view the Eucharist in this light, we ought to be cautious in following them. It seems to presuppose a false doctrine of the atonement, and has often obscured other more basic, eucharistic truths. The Eucharist is a giving. We give bread and wine, we give time and thought, we dedicate our work, we dedicate ourselves. We can call it a sacrifice. But if we do, we should understand it in terms of the definition which St Augustine gives in the tenth book of *The City of God* (X. 6): 'A true sacrifice is any act that is done in order that we may cleave in holy union to God'.

When the reformers were trying to reformulate their understanding of the Eucharist, Luther stuck on the words Jesus actually used, '*Hoc est corpus meum*', and felt impelled to continue construing the Eucharist in terms of substance and things. But

Jesus did not actually say *Hoc est corpus meum*, nor even *touto esti to soma mou*. What words he actually used we cannot say for certain, since we do not know whether he would have spoken in Hebrew or in Aramaic at the Last Supper. But in either case, the words he used—*zeh beśari* or *den biśri*—would not have carried the connotations of corporal substance that the words *Hoc est corpus meum* did for the Schoolmen. The words that came over into Greek as *soma* would often have been more a reflexive pronoun, myself, *emauton*, in the Semitic original. If we continue to translate our Lord's words as 'This is my body' we must give 'body' the sense it has in the words 'everybody' 'somebody' 'anybody', rather than the sense it bears in a coroner's court; and at present it could be better rendered by the slang phrase 'This is me', as said by an author pointing to a copy of his *magnum opus*, by an architect pointing to his masterpiece, a composer during a performance of his symphony, an Arnold or a Thring referring to his Rugby or his Uppingham.

When a person puts himself into his work or gives himself entirely to a cause or an institution, there is a sense both of achievement and of sacrifice. The work is what he has done and is the fulfilment of all his actions; but he has been able to accomplish it only at some cost. And so it was with Jesus Christ. In earthly terms the visible Church is our Lord's achievement, and the fellowship of Christ's religion is centred on the communion of its members with one another and with God in the sacred sharing of the bread and wine. In this sense, our Lord's words at the Last Supper, 'This is me', were the literal truth. The Communion service is Christ's doing. But at a greater cost. Christ instituted the Lord's Supper, and we continue to celebrate it, only because he then gave himself for us on the Cross, and was raised from the dead by the Father. He consecrated not only the bread, but the wine, and not only gave himself in the Thring sense, but gave his life in the literal sense. Body, *baśar*, *biśra*, may be understood in the sense of sacrifice; blood must. Christ's words mean not only that he is pouring his being into the Church constituted by the sharing of the Holy Communion, but that this can be so only because he is going to pour out his life on the Cross.

And this is the ultimate reason why Mass remains in some way factual, and simply exists as a kind of pure reality, separate from the weaving of our own thoughts. It is based on the fact of the crucifixion and the reality of the resurrection. Not only are we doing what our Lord commanded when he said 'Do this . . .', but it was in order that we should be able to commune with God and with one another that he came down from heaven, and each celebration of the Holy Communion is both an extension of Christ's achievement and a further expression of what it cost him,

et juges gratias de donis gratiae
beata referet plebs tibi, Domine,

to Whom also, together with God the Father and God the Holy Spirit, be ascribed all honour, power, dominion and might, henceforth and for ever, Amen.

(A very similar paper 'The Philosophical Background to Eucharistic Theology' is published as a chapter of *Thinking about the Eucharist* (London 1972) issued by the Doctrine Commission, to the members of which I am deeply indebted for what I publish here.

16 DOUBT

A Sermon

To those of you who are committed Christians, I shall have very little to say; I shall be talking to you who have not been able to make up your minds.

Some of you have come to believe in Christianity either in the course of this term or earlier, and some of you have not; you have tried; you went and listened to Bishop Huddleston, but his experience is not your experience; you argued, at coffee parties with your College Missioner, late into the night with your friends. And it has not come. You have found no convincing arguments to show that this world has been created by an omnipotent omniscient being who loves us, and gave his Son to live with us and die for us. You agree full well with Bishop Huddleston when he finds the civilization of Europe—our civilization—empty and absurd; you respect his overmastering conviction of the caring-ness of God. But you are not with him. You respect his experience, but you have not had it. In many ways you would like to have it, you would like to believe. But it would be dishonest to pretend that you are convinced by arguments which are not cogent. Wishful thinking never did achieve much; it certainly will not conjure God into existence, or raise again the man the Jews crucified. And so, as a matter of intellectual integrity, you cannot say that you are a Christian.

I do not think that this is wrong. It can be wrong, I know; it can be a pretext for pride, self-centred arrogance, and you will all have been warned of this, many many times; but doubt is far from being always pride. We know that we have only a short time to live, only a short time in which to decide what sort of life we ought to lead; we all feel, Christians and non-Christians alike, the urgent need to be redeeming the time; and yet many, often humble men of good will, find themselves unable to make a choice, unable to accept the good news that Christ came on earth to tell us.

And this is not surprising—not to a Christian. Because, it seems to me, the lack of conviction so many of our generation experience, is not, as is often assumed, a proof of not being a

Christian, but one of the trials of being a Christian, the trial that is most characteristic of our modern age.

We are not likely to be called to undergo the trials that the first Christians faced. Not many of you here are seriously likely to be killed for his sake; none of you will go to prison for confessing that Jesus is Lord; will any of us ever be really hungry? We, living in a land that flows with the waters of plenteousness, will never know thirst in the crude, physical sense; and though we may yet yearn for righteousness and truth, we as citizens of this country and members of this University, have our thirst slaked by deep draughts of justice and knowledge. Few graduates of Oxford will receive the call to martyrdom. Most of you will, quite rightly, take positions which call for patience rather than heroism, positions essential for the maintenance of our highly complicated society, positions which will be well rewarded with the good things our society has to offer. We fare sumptuously every day, and are clothed, if not in purple, at least in very substantial tweeds.

And yet, are we happy? 'Blessed are the poor, for they do not have to think', wrote Tolstoy in *War and Peace*. Do we not all sometimes look back with longing on the simpler certainties of an earlier age? I want to argue not that the Ages of Faith were all that we sometimes think they were, but as we have become more and more in control of our material environment, so we have become more and more conscious of our spiritual needs. Men seldom now can find companionship in shared adversity, and so man is lonely: it no longer now demands all his energies to secure the bare means of survival, and so he finds his leisured life full of futility.

As we have become more and more in control of our material environment, so we have become more and more conscious of our spiritual needs: the more we know of ourselves, the less sure we are: the more time we have had to be alone with our thoughts, the less we have liked it. Blessed are the poor, for they do not have to think.

It is an age of doubt. And it seems to me that doubt is the form in which many Christians in the present age are called upon to share in the sufferings of mankind after the example of our Lord. And the reason why so many Christians are unable to believe is just this: that doubt is the Cross that Christians of today are called to bear.

It is likely then that those Christians whom Christ is calling to share in his sufferings, are going to be called not in the way they had expected, not to some spectacular life of heroism or death of martyrdom, but to the secret agony of indecision, the silent torture of separation. It was as much in the Garden as on the Cross that Christ showed us what was in store for us, and showed that he was at one even with modern, intellectual, sceptical man: and any Christian who is serious in his professed willingness to participate in the passion of our Lord, must be prepared to go to Gethsemane as well as Golgotha, and to be called not to martyrdom but to wrestle with unknown doubts and strange horrors in the dark night of the soul.

> And Jacob was left alone; and there wrestled a man with him until the breaking of the day.　　　　　　　　　Gen. 32.24

It is not a new thing, doubt, but it has taken a new form. Our ancestors in the seventeenth century were racked with doubt, but they doubted whether God loved them or whether he had predestined them to perdition. We do not doubt that God, if he exists, loves us, and we are not distressed about the exact details of the Creed. Our doubt is whether there is a God at all, or whether we are merely chance collocations of molecules, who happen to be conscious, and are cursed with immortal longings and limited lives, infinite aspirations and finite abilities. This doubt, the most radical of all, is the one left for our age to face and to endure.

You may ask, 'Why? Why this agony, this waste, this ineffectiveness of doubt? Why does not God, if he really exists and really loves us, why does he not disclose himself more clearly to us, and set our minds at rest?'

Part of the answer is that it would not be consonant with our freedom for us to know God with coercive certainty. God has disclosed all he can of himself; enough, to enable us to respond to his love by loving him in return; not so much as to compel us to respond to his might by calculating that it would be in our own interests to conform willy-nilly to his wishes. Just as parents sometimes have to detach themselves from their children's affairs in order not to suffocate them with an ever-present love, so God hides himself enough to give us, his creatures, room to develop and be ourselves, and takes care not to stifle our little independences with a sort of celestial smother-knowledge.

I want to add to this a second consideration. It is only by long sojourning in the spiritual wilderness that some people can come to want God as he ought to be wanted. Christians and non-Christians alike fall short in this respect. The settled Christian, who believes, is perpetually taking God for granted. However humble the realization of God's grace makes him at first, it is almost impossible for this humility not, by slow and insensible steps, to be converted into pride. Those of you here tonight who *have* come to put their faith in Christ 'take heed lest ye fall'.

The non-Christians too have gone wrong in their idea of God. They have identified him with the Establishment, the God of the Pharisees, a God of restrictions and inhibitions, of dead respectability rather than of freedom and life. They have felt an immense sense of emancipation, when they realized that God, this God, did not exist. 'Have you not heard', says Nietzsche, 'that God is dead?' and this, not the resurrection, has been the good news for countless men and women of our time as they have grown to adulthood. 'God is dead', they have sung, 'and now we are free to enjoy ourselves, to make love and fornicate, and do as we like, and be ourselves, and no longer be restricted and confined by outworn shibboleths and deadening decalogues.' This is the song, the new song, the song of our age, which we have all heard sung, and whose music, whether we will it or not, is always ringing in our ears. And this is the sin, the sin of our age, for which we are all paying the penalty, in *angst* and *ennui* and boredom, in pointlessness, alienation and despair, not because God wants to punish us, but because it is the only remedy; it is only through long exile by the waters of Babylon, that we shall hang up our harps and shake off this song, and shall *want* to sing the Lord's song, and shall want there to be a Lord to sing to, a Lord to love and to be loved by.

This then is why God lets you doubt. It is so that you can rediscover that the gospel is *good* news, news which you really and truly want to hear, want to be true. Wishful thinking you thought Christianity was? You have to think this first, before you can welcome it wholeheartedly; until you are ready to love God, you are not ready to know him. This is not to say that when you think you are ready to love God, you will know him, or that by wanting it you can make the gospel true. The Wise Men had far to go, even after they had seen the star, and you too may find that you will have to spend many years in the wilderness, perhaps most of your life, seeking and searching, before you finally find yourself at the end of your travels and where there is peace for your soul.

It is not for me to tell you what the journey will be like: I could not even if I would. For that you must go to the writings of the saints and seers: St Paul, St Augustine, John Bunyan, perhaps Dostoievsky. My task is only to put in modern idiom the instructions for the first few steps. What is it then, to set out, not believing, in search for something you do not know whether it exists? and how are you to set about it? You are, in a way already showing faith, in the way that Abraham did, when he set out from Ur. You are sticking your neck out, running the risk that you may be wrong, that there may be nothing at the end of it to discover, except that there was nothing. To this extent then, you are already showing faith. You are also making yourselves vulnerable.

You are also making yourselves vulnerable. For Christianity teaches that God exists, that there is a Being who knows and cares what we do; and therefore it matters what we do. This is one of the key differences between the experience of the Christian and the experience of the atheist. For the Christian, everything matters. It has significance, because however much it may be forgotten by men, it is known to God, and God cares. And if once we are touched by the Christian gospel, it matters to us whether it matters or not. We lay ourselves open to caring—we come to care desperately whether there is a God or not, whether all our doings are known and valued, or whether they are all trivial and futile. And this is part of being a Christian, to be vulnerable, to care. Christ cared; and was wounded for our transgressions. And, as the mystery of the passion teaches us, it is only through the endless vulnerability of infinite caringness that we could be made whole. By his stripes we are healed. It was because God cared that he gave his Son, and it is only by caring too, that you can follow Christ, only by caring that you can accept the good news he came to give us.

What then are you to do, if you find yourself drawn to Christ but unable to believe that he is the Son of the living God, if you find yourself, as many people do, a New Testament agnostic? You should do as Descartes, the philosopher, did, who found himself doubting and who resolved to maintain all the practices of the Christian religion, while pursuing his method of philosophical doubt to the utmost. We can pray, even if we cannot always believe. We can say our prayers, we can read the Bible, we can go to church, we can try to conform our lives, often without success, but sometimes in little things with some small measure of success, to the pattern of Christian love. In this University, for instance, each one of you can decide not to make some catty remark, not to break some confidence, not to tell some amusing but untrue piece of gossip, not to turn a clever but cruel phrase about another man. All these things are things which we *can* do. We may not be able to believe, we may not be able honestly to commit ourselves to the whole Christian religion, but we can, quite honestly and with complete integrity, choose to do these things. Faith comes from God, and may not have come to you yet; but though you cannot be a believer just by choosing, you can be a doer just by choosing; though you cannot be a Christian, you can by a settled determination of the will be a would-be Christian. By trying to lead the Christian life, and by thinking out the Christian religion and its implications and by thinking out the alternatives and their implications—think out for example the materialist creed, 'I believe in matter', which ends 'and I believe in the meaninglessness of life, in the dissolution of the body and the death everlasting'—by thinking these out, by doing what you can of Christianity and wrestling with what you cannot, the doubts, the difficulties, the futility and the loneliness, you will be making yourselves to become Christians, to come to know the glory of God and his love towards us. It may take a long time. The Wise Men had far to go, and clever men of all times have been able to discern, and be beset by, difficulties that have been mercifully hid from the eyes of the unlearned and simple.

The way will not be easy or broad: Christ himself said that it would not. It may take you through desolate regions of experience, where no water is, but only the nausea that the existentialists know so well. And there is no guarantee that you will come out at the other end. But if you want to be a Christian, you must be prepared to take up your cross and follow Christ, follow him if necessary to Gethsemane, if necessary to Golgotha, if necessary in agony, if necessary in doubt; and be prepared, as Christ was, to trust in God even when not convinced of him. You too may have to say, 'Eloi, Eloi, lama, sabachthani'; but can you demand that you should be put to any lesser test?

125

17   SAYING THE CREEDS

The first Christians did not say the Creeds. They believed in Jesus, and believed many things about Jesus, but had no occasion to make a formal profession of faith. Jesus was present with them in the flesh. There was no doubt whom they were following, and though they only gradually came to understand why, it was because they recognized Jesus as the Christ, the Messiah, the Son of the living God (Matt. 16. 16, 14. 33). In the Apostolic age it was different. The name of Jesus was a common one, and it was necessary to distinguish Jesus who was born of Mary from Jesus the son of Sirach, Jesus of Nazareth from the many Joshuas who lived in Galilee at that time, the true Messiah who was executed by the Romans but rose again on the third day from the many false messiahs who talked big but did nothing, or who led abortive revolts against the Romans and paid the price for insurrection. We, at the end of the second millennium of the Christian era, do not feel the same need to secure identity of reference when we use the word 'Jesus': there is only one person we could be referring to, and we all have some idea of who he is and what he did. But even so there are occasions, as in ordinary secular life, when it is well to supplement a bare name with an address or a description: we always might need to make it clear that we believed in Jesus of Nazareth, and not some leader of a southern Californian sect who had taken the same name.

Modern theologians often make the point that we believe *in* God, rather than believe *that* certain propositions are true. It is a valid and important point, but is easily misunderstood as meaning that Christians do not have to have any beliefs *that* at all. But we cannot believe in God without believing that he exists, and we cannot believe in Jesus without believing that certain things are true of him. Our descriptions of Jesus—as the Messiah, the Son of God, the one who died for us, the man who was raised from the dead—serve not only to make it clear in whom we are putting our trust, but also to give some of our reasons for trusting in him. And merely to give these descriptions is enough to constitute a profession of faith, as when Peter first said, 'You are the Messiah, the

Son of the living God' (Matt. 16. 16). Thus belief *in* presupposes some sort of belief *that*, and to express a belief *that* often constitutes an acknowledgement of a belief *in*. Nevertheless, there is a difference, and the early Christians were more concerned with believing in than believing that. In particular, when converts came to be baptized, it was natural for them to put into words their commitment to Christ in some form or other. Many different formulae are to be found in the New Testament which may have been used as baptismal professions of faith. They are not all the same, nor is there any reason why they should be. Christ comes to us in many different ways, and different Christians will emphasize different aspects of what he means to us. To one he is the liberator from sin, to another the man who can end our separation from God, to another he is God made man, to another the person who gave himself on the Cross, to another the priest who bids us share in the sacred feast. These different emphases need not be incompatible with one another. We believe in the same God, and would acknowledge many of the same reasons. But we stress different strands in our understanding, and in so far as we formulate our faith in words, we may well work it out in different ways.

Although many different ways of articulating one's faith are acceptable, they are not all equally valid, nor are all of them even acceptable. Many have said 'Lord, Lord' without really following in the Way. I cannot honestly say 'I believe in Jesus' unless I believe him to have been telling the truth about himself; and therefore I cannot be a follower of Jesus, as I might be of Socrates or Bertrand Russell, believing him just to be a good man whose example I wish to imitate. One of the distinguishing parts of Jesus' teaching was the fatherhood of God, and that he was, in some special sense, the Son of God; from the time of our Lord's ministry on earth, to commit oneself to him was to trust in the Father and to recognize Jesus as the Son of God. Any profession of faith which did not include this much was not a genuine commitment to Christ. Herod believed Jesus was a great miracleworker and wanted to see him, but was not on that account a Christian, and there are many people today who believe Jesus was a great man, and that his influence is still capable of working psychological miracles, but who are not what we should reckon as believers in Christ. Different people have different understandings of Jesus and different commitments towards him, and not all these

constitute the faith which saves a person from himself and enables
him to be admitted into the fellowship of Christ's religion. We
have to distinguish within the wide variety of beliefs about Jesus
and the range of beliefs in him, those that constitute Christian
faith from those that do not. And that is why we had to have
creeds. Creeds are formulae for distinguishing the family of Christian beliefs from other, possibly para-Christian, ones. To some extent they may be likened to the bones which are fleshed out by
each person's individual understanding of the faith. But with the
passage of time they became a set of criteria for picking out true
Christian faiths from non-Christian ones. And hence they are
determined not only by Christian truth but by prevalent error. In
the pagan world there were many gods. It was not enough to say
that Jesus was the Son of God—so was Hercules; it was
necessary to exclude the possibility that God the Father was only
one among many Gods, or that, like Plato's Demiurge, he had
rather restricted powers: 'I believe in *one* God. . . .' 'I believe in
God the Father *Almighty*, maker of heaven and earth. . . .' We in
the twentieth century are not tempted to be polytheists, nor are
we tempted to be docetists, monophysites, Arians or Nestorians.
We are tempted, rather, to be atheists, materialists, determinists,
Marxists, or Freudians, and therefore we should pick on a quite
different set of tenets as characteristic of the Christian position.
We believe in the existence of God, the openness of being, the
freedom of the will, the importance of non-economic factors, and
the responsibility of man. Against the background of modern unbelief we can formulate what is peculiar to the Christian understanding and distinguishes it from its contemporary rivals, and
often we feel impatient at the frequent repetition of the formulae
of former days: 'being of one substance with the Father'; 'he
descended into hell'; 'who proceedeth from the Father and the
Son'; 'the resurrection of the body'. Some churchmen feel that we
ought, if not exactly to drop the Creeds, at least to lower them
below the threshold of consciousness. Others feel very defensive,
and that if one jot or tittle of the Chalcedonian definitions were
ever omitted, we should thereby be showing that we are no longer
firm in the faith. But such a controversy largely rests on a mis-
understanding of what the Creeds originally were, and what part
they now play in Anglican worship. The Creeds are not, and could
not be, a full exposition of Christian doctrine. Nor are they a

natural vehicle for preaching the gospel. Nor do they now constitute those essential propositions which a man must affirm if he is not to be damned everlastingly. Rather, they arose naturally out of the needs of the Church, and they retain their position in our worship partly as a matter of historical piety, partly because although we no longer have to face the same problems as the early Church, the way they solved those problems still has much to teach us.

Creeds seem much less open to objection than we sometimes casually assume. Of course no modern man would naturally find himself saying that Christ was any sort of substance at all, let alone 'one substance with the Father'. The word 'substance' has entirely changed its meaning in the intervening centuries, and now is seldom used by anyone except chemists. But if the question is put, couched in terms of fourth-century Greek philosophy, then it would be much less wrong to say that Christ was of one substance with the Father—i.e. that he really was God—than that he was not of one substance with the Father—i.e. that he was just a good man. And so in general with statements of doctrine. They are not to be understood as though they were propositions of geography or mathematics, whose meaning is perfectly clear, just the same in this context as in any other, and either entirely true or else entirely false. Rather, they should be seen as the least inadequate way of expressing a truth which surpasses human telling, and that their meaning is given as much by what they deny as by what they seem to be literally asserting. In particular, the Creeds were fashioned against the foil of contrary opinions, and their meaning is to be understood only in the context of the assumptions which were then being taken for granted and in contrast to the alternatives which were being excluded. With the passage of time, as old questions were settled and new ones raised, the old questions would cease to be such burning issues, and would cease to mean so much to contemporary churchmen. They became like the battle-songs of yesteryear, which we still sing, but for different reasons and with a different understanding from what had once been the case. All in all we think the Church has been providentially guided down the ages, and that it was right to make it clear how the Christian faith differed from Gnosticism, Montanism, Donatism, and the other misinterpretations which once seemed likely to overwhelm it. When we sing the Nicene Creed at the Eucharist we are identifying with the Church in its struggle to elucidate and present the pure word of God down the ages, and for many people it is entirely right and natural so to do. But just because of the change in our conceptual structure, in the meaning of words, and in the burning issues of the day, other people find the Creeds ossified and alien, and feel uncomfortable about being asked to recite them in public worship. It is therefore necessary to go back to their original purpose and function, and reassess the part they ought to play in the worship of the Church today.

The first professions of faith were made at baptism, and it is still at baptism that some form of credal affirmation seems most naturally called for. The individual is turning to Christ, and needs to avow his commitment as he enters into Christ's body. The traditional creeds are criticized because they seem too propositional, too theological, when what is wanted is something more personal, less intellectual. Though once it may have been necessary to guard against false identifications and ancient heresies, now it is no longer so. The words 'Jesus Christ' now refer to only one person, and in the context of a Church service there can be no doubt where the new Christian is putting his trust. Moreover, some intelligent seekers after Christ have difficulty in accepting some clauses of the Creed as they understand them—if they do not believe in hell, how can they say that Jesus descended into hell?—and the one thing the Church wants to be sure of at baptism is that any commitment made shall be made from the bottom of the heart and with complete intellectual integrity. Hence, it is argued, the profession of faith should not be made in the terms of some antiquated creed, whose terms are either not fully understood, or else not fully believed but rather in words which flow naturally from the heart, and which can be affirmed *ex animo* by modern man.

There is much force in this contention—for those who feel it. A modern Christian may, like the Ethiopian eunuch, be properly baptized without first saying the Apostles' Creed. It is better that a man should profess his faith in the simpler form of the Series 2 baptism service than that he should say the Apostles' Creed but with a number of mental reservations. Nevertheless it does not follow from this that we should go further and drop every form of credal affirmation. For the Christian religion does have cognitive content. It rests upon certain historical facts and implies certain sorts of views about the world. It would be a mockery for a man to seek for baptism if he did not believe in the existence of God, or held there never was a Jesus of Nazareth. Exactly what views about God and about the historical Jesus are, or are not, compatible with the Christian faith is a matter on which we have less inclination, and less need, to be dogmatic than the early Christians. It might be right to refer difficult cases to the bishop, who could examine by question and answer any candidate that felt unable to affirm any official creed, and could then decide whether or not he should be accepted for baptism—always bearing in mind that both for the Church's sake and for the individual's it is sometimes necessary to say 'No; you are not a Christian yet. We can only pray that you may be led to a knowledge of Christ in time to come.' In the other cases, where the bishop found the candidate's beliefs to be consonant with the Christian religion, the candidate should make his profession of faith in his own words approved by the bishop, and this would be enough to ensure the genuineness of his Christian commitment.

Although in some difficult cases it would be right not to insist upon traditional, or even on any official, forms of credal affirmation, it does not follow that the Apostles' Creed should not be generally used at baptism, and there are some arguments in favour of keeping it. For many people, the knowledge of Christ is mediated through the Church, and the Christ to whom they are committing themselves is the Christ to whom the Church bears witness; by using the traditional forms we emphasize the historicity of the Church, and articulate the fact that the Church into which the newly baptized Christian will be admitted is the same Church as the Church of the Fathers which formulated the Creeds. The average Christian does not have a very clear or detailed idea of the content of his faith. If pressed, he might well end up by saying that he believed the same as the Archbishop of Canterbury, whatever that might be. But unclarity over details and inarticulateness in theology are not disqualifications for entering into the Kingdom of heaven. The average Christian may not be good at thinking things out for himself, but he is not particularly called to do so, and may well follow his Christian vocation in entirely traditional forms as mediated to him by the Church. Even if of an enquiring turn of mind he may still say *Credo ut intelligam*, and give his loyalty to a whole intellectual

131

tradition before he has worked it out and understood each separate part of it for himself. It often happens in secular life. Young men are attracted to, and declare their adherence to, Absolute Idealism, Neo-Kantianism, or Logical Positivism, long before they have verified and validated each separate tenet of these schools for themselves. And for many people the natural and proper way of expressing their loyalty to Christ is in the traditional profession of faith which the Church formulated long ago and has handed down from generation to generation. They do not pretend to understand the full significance of every phrase in the Creed: but it is through the Church's understanding that they have come to know Christ, and in terms of it that their commitment can best be spelt out. For these reasons the traditional formulation of the Apostles' Creed ought not to be abandoned. But it would emphasize the role of the Apostles' Creed as the expression of the Church's understanding of the faith if the actual words used were in the mouth of the minister not the candidate for baptism, and if the candidate expressed the personal nature of the God in whom he believed. Instead of the candidate reciting the Apostles' Creed, the minister should ask him 'Do you believe in God the Father Almighty, Maker of heaven and earth?', and the candidate should answer 'I believe and trust *in him*'; and then 'Do you believe in Jesus Christ . . . ?', etc.

Creeds are not only said at Baptism. As we have seen, the 'Nicene' Creed was originally a conciliar creed, recited by bishops to express the corporate view of the whole Church. The original form was in the first person plural, we believe, *pisteuomen*, but it is familiar to us in the Communion service in the first person singular. 'I believe in one God, the Father. . . .' We also say the Apostles' Creed at Mattins and Evensong and according to the rubric of the Book of Common Prayer should say the Athanasian Creed once a month at Mattins. In many churches the Athanasian Creed is, in fact, not said: many churchmen feel unhappy at affirming that anyone who does not keep the Catholic faith whole and undefiled will, without doubt, perish everlastingly. A smaller number have qualms at reciting even the Nicene or Apostles' Creed, not necessarily because they actually doubt the truth of any of the propositions contained therein, but rather because they feel it gives too mechanical and propositional a form to the faith. Other churchmen feel very much the reverse. For some of them the Creeds are canticles, more glorious than the Gloria, more joyful than the Jubilate, expressing the Christian's triumphant affirmation of the truth about God, man, and the world, and manifesting his solidarity with the Church throughout the ages. The Creeds are to be sung rather than said. Others are more defensive. They believe that Christianity is concerned with what is true, and that unless certain things are true, the Christian religion must fall—

> Had Christ that once was slain
> Ne'er burst his three day prison
> Our faith had been in vain . . .

and therefore they resist any attempt to reduce the propositional commitment of the individual Christian. This seems to have been one of the reasons why the Synod rejected the suggestion of reverting in Series 3 to the first person plural form of the Nicene Creed. Behind these attitudes lie two views about doctrine, both of which express important aspects of the truth, but neither capable of capturing the whole complexity of Christian truth. In fact, both in different ways fail to do justice to the implications of the incarnation.

One view, which for reasons that will emerge, will be called the Judaistic view, holds that Christian faith and Christian morals have been revealed by God through Christ to mankind, and it is the plain duty of the individual Christian to believe what God has shown to be the truth about him and to do what God has shown to be his will for us. We should believe that the Holy Ghost proceeds from the Father for much the same reasons and in exactly the same spirit as we believe that we should keep the Sabbath day holy. The merit of this view is that it emphasizes the transcendence of God and the independence of God. God is not just a creature of our own imaginings, and the truth of God is something quite separate from whether we believe it or not. God is something other than us, and our opinions about him are to be judged by whether they conform to the facts about him, rather than theological truth to be fashioned to fit such feelings we happen to have. Only if we approach God in this spirit can we come to know him and he save us. But if we stress the otherness of God too much we create an alienation between God and man and it becomes impossible for man ever to be at one with God.

Although a conscientious man may fulfil the moral law scrupulously and believe everything he has been told about God, neither his actions nor his intellectual attitudes will be authentically his own. They have been imposed from outside, and will come to be felt as an external yoke which confines or denies the development of the individual rather than something which fulfils it. This had happened so far as the moral law was concerned in Judaism in the time for our Lord, and Jesus criticized the Scribes and Pharisees not on account of what they actually did but because their actions were dead and external to their real selves. In the Christian era theology has sometimes similarly gone dead on us—most notably at the end of the Scholastic period and perhaps now in our own age. If morals or theology are made external to us, they will ossify and die. If man is to do the will of God, or believe the truth about God, entirely whole-heartedly, he must come to it of himself, and must therefore be able to identify with God. No Jew could identify with Jehovah—the very idea was blasphemy. But we can identify with Jesus. This is why it was necessary for God to be made man, and come down from heaven for us and our salvation. And although it is quite right to maintain that there are truths about God which we ought to believe, if we set too rigid an insistence on doctrinal orthodoxy, we may be guilty of worshipping creeds rather than worshipping Christ, and of understanding God as a god who could reveal himself on Sinai but not in the life and suffering of his Son Jesus.

The other view, which will be called the Existentialist view, holds that Christian faith is merely the articulation of the intellectual attitudes of the individual who seeks to follow Christ. In the course of his discipleship he may find it helpful to think of God as a Father or a Creator, or think of Christ as risen or ascended, but the real meaning of these formulae is simply what they mean to him. If traditional forms of affirmation are helpful, then certainly they should be retained. But otherwise the individual Christian is to be free to affirm other things, as the Spirit moves him. What is important is not that he should give lip service to ancient articles of faith but that he should be honest with himself and sincere in all his sayings. The merit of this view is that it emphasizes the immanence of God and the operation of the Holy Spirit. We are guided by God along different pathways into different understandings of the truth. Each ought to follow his own light, in intellectual as well as moral matters, and honest error is often more illuminating than insincere correctitude. Only if a man is true to himself can he be true to others or true to the Truth. But if we stress too much the way in which God is to be found within us, we shall end by simply identifying God with the individual, and losing all sense of God's being distinct from his creatures. In morals too great an emphasis on individualism led to antinomianism, and in questions of knowledge and belief it leads to subjectivism. Honest error may be preferable to dishonest avowals, but it is error nonetheless, and unless the possibility of being wrong is fully recognized no moral and no intellectual progress will be made. It is not, and cannot be, enough that we each should do what is right in his own eyes, and my believing something to be so is necessarily different from whether it actually is so or not. More specifically, too extreme a doctrine of the inner light also denies the need for the incarnation. If the Holy Spirit could make each one of us a prophet, there would have been no need for Jesus to live among us. If it was for us and for our salvation that he came down from heaven, was crucified under Pontius Pilate and rose again the third day, then these facts are true and are importantly true irrespective of whether an individual feels like affirming them. There is a givenness about Christ which is an essential part of Christian truth but which is implicitly denied by the existentialist account. Whatever we believe about Christian belief, we must believe that it is important to believe that Christ actually was born a man, did live among us, was crucified and did rise again.

18 NON CREDO

1. I do not believe in phenomenalism or solipsism. My experiences are not the only things to exist, but are essentially experiences of some other more important reality. Other things and other persons exist independently of me.

2. I do not believe in materialism. Things are not the only things to exist. Natural phenomena possess a pattern that is rational and can be discovered. The laws of nature are not opaque uniformities but are the manifestations of a creative mind. The ultimate reality is neither a mathematical formula nor a brute fact, but a person.

3. I do not believe in determinism. Men can choose between alternatives, and their choice is not determined either by the stars or by their genes or by their environment or by their psychological make-up. These and other factors restrict the range of alternatives available to the agent and may influence his decision, but do not always remove all possibility of choice. Each man is responsible for what he decides to do. And, in particular, it matters what I do.

4. I do not believe in irrationalism, emotivism, pragmatism, or subjectivism. Actions can be justified on rational grounds, and such justifications are not reducible to explanations in psychological or physiological terms but are valid in their own right. Values are objective, and although they need to be affirmed and authenticated by each man, they are not merely the expression of his feeling or a means of influencing others, and it is quite possible for a man to be sincere but wrong in his moral beliefs.

5. I do not believe in Marx or Freud. Money and sex are important, but not all-important. There are other objectives, more worth pursuing, which men can, and sometimes do, aim for. In particular, personal relationships are more important than either economic or sexual ones. Human beings need fellowship to fulfil themselves, but often cannot find it on account of their own unlikeableness, or because they forsake it in the pursuit of lesser goods.

6.   I do not believe in man. Human achievements, although sometimes great, are always transient: human insights, although occasionally profound, are often wrong. All men are liable to self-centredness, and some are insanely selfish. Wickedness flourishes, and even high-minded idealism is easily turned to evil ends. The history of man has not been happy. Institutions grow corrupt, and change is often for the worse.

7.   I do not believe in morality very much. Men ought to be moral, but most of those that are moral are moral for the wrong reasons and are pretty miserable about it. It is one of the merits of Christ's religion that his yoke is easy and his burden light. Instead of the austere impersonality of the categorical imperative, we are invited to identify with our fellow men who are, like us, sons of God and joint heirs with Christ. The morality which flows from this attitude is spontaneous and authentic, not cramping or cold.

8.   I do not believe in self-help or self-improvement. I am what I am thanks to the generosity and affection of others, and could not achieve anything without their continuing aid and support. I want to be united with others, and share my aspirations and activities with them. More especially I want to be united with Jesus by being a member of his corporate body, and through him be at one with God, which I could not even begin to be by any other means. I cannot force intimacy with any person, and so cannot of myself alone achieve any personal relationship with anybody else, but must always depend on the willingness of others to have me. In particular, knowledge of God is no achievement of mine but a favour of his, something given rather than got, to be accepted with gratitude, not taken for granted or presumed upon.

9.   I do not believe in demythologizing, or in the impossibility of miracles, or in cutting down the Gospel stories to suit the preconceptions of the modern mind. I do not believe that Jesus was just a good man, or that his life and works are just the fabrication of the early Church, or that he could not have done the wonderful works attributed to him by the Evangelists and the writers of the Epistles, or that he failed to rise from the dead, or that the resurrection is to be understood in some sophisticated or Pickwickian sense. Jesus was a man, of like passions with

ourselves, who is therefore one of us, who knows what it is like to be a man, and what the human predicament really amounts to. But Jesus is also divine. His words and deeds reveal the divine nature more directly and more authoritatively than do those of any other prophet; and especially, in giving up his life, he made manifest to us the nature and costliness of love, and the fact that God is love, and loves us men without term or limit.

10. I do not believe that death is the end of everything. I do not know what lies beyond the grave, and I sense formidable philosophical difficulties in the popular idea of a continuing consciousness unbroken by death. But the Christian life is a continual reaching out to the future, which would be incoherent if the future were blank; and it does not seem consonant with what Christ told us of the Father to suppose that he has nothing in store for us, or would snuff us out when this life is ended.